ORDINARY WONDER TALES

Ordinary Wonder Tales

Essays

Emily Urquhart

BIBLIOASIS

Windsor, Ontario

FIRST EDITION
10 9 8 7 6 5 4 3 2 1

Library and Archives Canada Cataloguing in Publication
Title: Ordinary wonder tales / Emily Urquhart.
Names: Urquhart, Emily, author.
Identifiers: Canadiana (print) 20220256853 | Canadiana (ebook) 20220257000 | ISBN 9781771965057 (softcover) | ISBN 9781771965064 (ebook)
Subjects: LCGFT: Essays.
Classification: LCC PS8641.R684 O73 2022 | DDC C814/.6—dc23

Edited by Daniel Wells
Copyedited by Cat London
Typeset by Vanessa Stauffer
Cover and interior illustrations by Byron Eggenschwiler

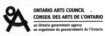

Published with the generous assistance of the Canada Council for the Arts, which last year invested $153 million to bring the arts to Canadians throughout the country, and the financial support of the Government of Canada. Biblioasis also acknowledges the support of the Ontario Arts Council (OAC), an agency of the Government of Ontario, which last year funded 1,709 individual artists and 1,078 organizations in 204 communities across Ontario, for a total of $52.1 million, and the contribution of the Government of Ontario through the Ontario Book Publishing Tax Credit and Ontario Creates.

PRINTED AND BOUND IN CANADA

[An] alternative term for "fairy tale" is "wonder tale" from the German *Wundermärchen*, and it catches a quality of the genre more eloquently than "fairy tale" or "folk tale." Although it does not enjoy the currency of "fairy tale," "wonder tale" recognizes the ubiquitousness of magic in the stories.

MARINA WARNER,
Once Upon a Time:
A Short History of Fairy Tales

Every narrator reinvents the tale.

JOAN ACOCELLA,
"Once Upon a Time: The Lure
of the Fairy Tale," The New Yorker

For Rory

Contents

The Matter

THE YEAR THAT I TURNED three I slept in a bedroom that was known to be haunted. Returning to that room now, in memory, I am a bystander looking in through an open doorway at a young girl lying in a sleigh bed with a tall headboard. She is yellow-haired and motionless, wearing a flannel nightgown. She holds the neck of a small plush lamb in the curl of her palm. The sheets on her bed are white and aglow in the blackness of the night room. The air is chilled and still. The child has many blankets on her bed to keep her warm. She appears to be asleep. I enter the room and move closer to the child. I see her blink. She is awake, her gaze fixated on a spot overhead. This is where the inky fluid mass has materialized, seeping in from the corner of the room above where the bed has been snugged against the wall. She has not seen a stingray in her life, but when she does, twenty years from now in the Caribbean, she will recognize something in the ocean creature, in its darkness and its size and also in its rippled movement. The ink blot is made of air, or water, or maybe gas. Some might argue that it is conjured of mind or spirit, but to the small girl, it is matter. It is part of the physical universe. There is no urgency to its visit. It bides its time as it quivers in the dark, making its presence silently known, but eventually, as she knows it will, the inky mass speaks to her in a breathy hiss. It declares itself in a language that is either French or English or some other form of communication that is not linguistic. It says, every time, Emily, go get your mother. The small girl does not move. I don't move now. Across the years between us—forty-three—we remain stilled in fear.

The haunted bedroom was in an eighteenth-century stone house in the small village of Flavigny-sur-Ozerain in Burgundy, France, where I lived with my mother and father during the year my father was on sabbatical from his job as a professor of fine arts. The house belonged to my father's colleague Virgil Burnett, an artist who was a professor in the same department as my father, and his wife, Anne, who was a classics scholar. They had two daughters, Maud and Melissa, who were about a decade older than I was. The Burnetts lived in the house in France part-time when Virgil and Anne were not teaching, and the rest of the year they offered their home to a roster of academics and artists and their families.

My mother tells me that moving to Flavigny was like time travel. The house sits in the centre of a walled medieval village set high on a hill. It has a working seminary. Young monks in black robes wandered the cobblestone streets and played soccer in the meadow at the edge of town just off a trail that led to an ancient but still working stone washhouse. Every home in the village came with a garden plot outside the wall. Farmers shepherded their cattle through an eleventh-century stone gate every morning, returning home before sunset. Only some streets were passable by car. Later, when I began studying folklore, Flavigny was the place my mind conjured when the hero set off on a long journey: after passing through the medieval gates, they would descend into the Burgundian hills and disappear into their quest.

My parents slept in the master bedroom on the second floor and my room was across the hall. The next closest bedroom was one floor above, in the attic. My mother remembers that the small room was set up for a child, with a single bed and a bookshelf stocked with children's literature such as Angela Banner's Ant and Bee books, Where the Wild Things Are by Maurice Sendak, and a French-language series about street cats of which I was particularly fond. The room was part of an addition that had been added in the early nineteenth century. It had one window that looked on to a walled-in garden. My bed was made of dark wood and was pushed into the corner opposite the window. At night, there was no ambient light. The village streetlights were extinguished at nine and this brought a darkness I'd never experienced before in my young life. Shadows and light depended on the moon cycle. We moved to Flavigny in August, 1979, when I was two years old. I began waking in the night soon after.

The French word for ghost is "revenant," meaning those who return from the dead, but the spirit that entered my room at night was not human. I never saw a face or discerned a person-like shape. Once, it visited in the form of a turtle named Skipper-Dee that lived in the garden. Most times it was a vague outline, darker than the darkness of the room. It vibrated with energy and had a fluid, inconsistent form. These visits elicited an emotion that I can best describe as a cross between solemnity and terror.

My nightmares persisted throughout the fall, prompting my mother to take me to see the doctor in Venarey-les-Laumes, the closest town. The doctor prescribed a suppository. The casual logic of this detail is one of my favourite plot points of this story. People have tried many bizarre ways to rid their spaces and bodies of unwanted spirits—acts of religious exorcism, smudging, throwing salt, or spitting—but this doctor felt it would be best cured with a rectal pill. My mother wasn't convinced. "I only gave you one of those," she told me. "French drugs were quite medieval at the time."

*

When I was a young child I believed in everything. The year we spent in France my parents took me to Lourdes, where we walked the stations of the cross and I believed that Jesus was stoned to death and that he came back to life. I believed in the Apparition of the Virgin Mary at the grotto and in the angels that soared across the domed ceilings of the churches we visited. My sole child companion during that period was an imaginary friend named Martha. She was a character from my favourite picture book, so I suppose I also believed that all the people, places, beings, and events in books were real, too.

I believed in fairies and in making wishes. I believed that my stuffed toy lamb was as alive as the stray black cat that hung around our front door yowling for his daily bowl of milk. If my parents had told me the cat was my younger sibling, I'd probably have believed this, too. I believed in everything that existed and everything that did not and in this way, based on studies of childhood beliefs over the past century, I was just like every other child my age.

Psychologist Jean Piaget was the first to study belief among the very young. He felt that children create their own understanding of the world based on discovery and discrepancy—a progression of continual adjustment that unfolds over a series of stages. It was his position that between the ages of two and seven all children engage in magical thinking. Much research on the topic has followed in his wake. Later studies showed that while children are inclined toward fantastical beliefs they do have a cognitive understanding of what is imaginary and what is real and that they're able to use reason and logic to draw these conclusions. For one study, researchers invented but did not define something called a "surnit" and presented two different scenarios for children to verify whether it was real or make-believe. Children who were told that a surnit helped doctors in hospitals reasonably concluded it was real. A story about ghosts catching surnits while they flew around at night was met with skepticism.

Children's beliefs lasted longer when reinforced by authority figures and, specifically, by their actions—putting out milk and cookies for Santa, or finding coins from the Tooth Fairy under a pillow. Christian children were more likely to view stories from the Bible as historic rather than fantastical, despite supernatural events such as Moses parting the Red Sea. If a child invented a mystical creature, they were more inclined to believe in its power. Based on this last finding, if the apparition in my bedroom was a figment of my imagination then it was all the more real, and more frightening, because I had conjured it myself.

My parents didn't tell me that ghosts were real, as they had with Santa Claus and the Tooth Fairy, only that I shouldn't be afraid. My mother wasn't sure if I was experiencing a haunting but she didn't rule it out. She said this was because she comes from an Irish family and they believe in ghosts, and, also, that they celebrate them. My father, who grew up in his family's funeral home, was accustomed to the thin line that separates the dead from the living. He never spoke of spirits or ghouls but the theme appeared in his paintings, sculptures, and drawings that often featured looming unknowable shapes that were almost realistic, but, at the same time, impossible. Mysterious and dark, some of these were not unlike what I saw in the small bedroom at night.

*

The suppository did not help and my night terrors persisted. I drew a picture of the apparition and showed it to my parents. In my drawing a small girl with yellow hair lies in a bed with a tall headboard, a dark scribble hovering above her. As with my memory of the spectral being, it was shapeless and non-human. It was not a see-through dead person, or a pale child, or a sheet with two holes cut out for eyes. It was none of the things that I would later learn to associate with ghosts and hauntings.

I was too young to categorize my experience, but even now I struggle to define what it was. Those who study supernatural belief face a similar dilemma. Deciding what constitutes a ghost is a problem for scholars, writes historian Kathryn Edwards in *A History of Ghosts in Early and Modern Europe: Research and Future Trajectories*. Pinning down her subject was daunting because "apparitions labelled as ghosts could be sound, movement, or sudden temperature shifts." There are also different types of hauntings. A person who appears to you in spirit at the time of their death is called a wraith. The "old hag" is what Newfoundlanders have named the sensation of waking to a person sitting on your chest. A poltergeist, which translates from German as noisy paired with the word ghost, is disruptive and sometimes violent. There are also benevolent hauntings, kindly spirits and helpful angels. My experience was none of these although I recognize elements within all of them.

I named my apparition Something's the Matter, which could stand as both definition and classification. I had used the word "matter," meaning a problem or concern. It had no doubt been posed to me as a question—*is something the matter?* But it could equally apply to matter as the term that describes our physical world, which is all that takes up space and is distinct from energy. Matter is everything that surrounds us. It is indisputable. No one can argue whether matter exists or not: it simply is. I believe this is what I was trying to communicate to my parents. I was naming a worrying event which was not just real to me, but tangible, observable. By illustrating my night terror I was telling my mother and father that this was something to be taken seriously. They seemed to understand the value and urgency of my message because they kept the drawing I made of the Something's the Matter and my father labelled and dated it for me in neat handwriting. It looks like something you'd find in a botanical textbook or in a museum, something you might pin in place and put behind glass.

*

In late fall of the year we spent in Flavigny my mother wrote to Virgil and Anne, updating them on our stay in their home and, as an aside, she mentioned my nightmares. In a return letter from Anne she learned that Virgil had also felt some disturbance in the small bedroom. It happened during the first summer they spent in the house. Maud was a baby at the time, asleep in the small bedroom, and Virgil had stepped in to check on her. As he passed through the door he felt a sinister cold spot. It had no explicable source. He felt uneasy leaving his sleeping child alone, so he fetched a pillow and blanket and spent the night on the floor beside Maud's bed. I remember Virgil with small round glasses, white hair and a beard, and that he often wore a suitcoat, so I envision him as a distinguished older man in spectacles and a smart jacket, wrapped in a sheet, asleep on the floor. It's not quite right, though, because he must have been a young man then. He might have had brown hair, and more of it than I remember.

Virgil remains the only adult who sensed a problem in the small bedroom. In her letter, Anne told my mother that the room was inhabited by a children's ghost. Not that it was the ghost of a child, but a spirit that only appeared to the very young. She wrote that a second child had suffered from a ghostly vision the year before we arrived. A Canadian artist named Walter Bachinski and his wife Annie had been living in the home with their two children Matthew and Sarah. My parents knew the Bachinskis well; in fact, it was through them that they first met, so it's possible my mother also heard this story directly from Annie. My mom couldn't remember the details when I asked her recently, but she thought it was the little girl who'd slept in the small bedroom. Of all the parents in the story of the ghost, only my mother and Walter are still alive. My mother suggested that I ask Walter about the haunted bedroom. She didn't have a contact for him, but felt I might find one through his artist website. "Maybe he could tell you more," she said. "I'm sure he will remember."

*

I often tell my two children the story of my haunting and their favourite part is when I describe the apparition as a turtle and imitate the creature's voice. I speak in the breathy hiss that I remember from childhood and my kids throw their heads back and laugh and ask me to do it again. *And what did you call it?* my son will ask, although he knows I named it Something's the Matter. He wants to hear me say it out loud. They find this part funny, too.

One summer afternoon, while I was eating lunch in the park with my children along with another neighbourhood mom and her son, my daughter asked me to tell the story of my ghost. My own children were five and nine. My friend's son was eight. We were eating kid food—cheese sandwiches, baby carrots, orange slices, and crackers shaped like goldfish. We'd planned to buy Popsicles for dessert. I began my story in the usual way, describing the ghost as a turtle named Skipper-Dee, and, encouraged by my children's laughter, emphasized its raspy voice.

Buoyed by my audience, I had overlooked the other family's reaction until my story concluded. The mother had turned her entire body towards her child so that her back was now facing me. It was as if she was shielding her son from physical harm. She was speaking to him in a low but audible voice, saying, *Ghosts aren't real. This is a made-up story. This never really happened.* Then, as an afterthought, which must have been meant for me, but sounded as if she were speaking to herself, she said, *I know some people have different beliefs about things, but…*

She trailed off and didn't finish her sentence. I could feel my face growing warm. My son continued to laugh, repeating the refrain himself now. *Go get your mother! Go get your mother!* He eventually tired of this, and the kids ate their sandwiches and goldfish crackers and vegetables and the conversation moved on to something more benign, the kind of acceptable park talk about where to buy bathing suits for children, what day camps still have spots available, which pools were open and when. I had trouble concentrating, not because the topics were boring, although they were, but because of the way I'd been shamed. I hadn't realized that the story was inappropriate or upsetting. I'd meant it to be entertaining, but instead my narrative prompted the child's mother to create a barrier between him and me and to contradict what I was saying. I was confused by her behaviour but also perplexed by my own. I'd crossed into taboo and broken social norms without any awareness. Later, replaying the incident, I wondered if the problem lay in the way I was telling the story.

Haunting narratives are dual stories because one listener might hear it as true while the other understands it to be fiction. It's a question of perception, and this is different from a fairy tale, which, from the outset, is understood as make-believe. In a chapter titled "Scientific Rationalism and Supernatural Experience Narratives" in *Haunting Experiences: Ghosts in Contemporary Folklore*, Diane Goldstein writes that when people describe personal supernatural experiences—namely, some form of haunting—they typically do so cautiously and with obvious embarrassment. They embed other possible explanations to prove that they themselves might not fully believe in the magic of their stories. *It could have been the wind*, they'll say, or *maybe it was a shadow*, or, the most self-damning of all, *it was probably all in my head*. The tellers include small unnecessary details to help build their case, as if on a witness stand. Unlike ghost stories, personal haunting narratives tend to be mono-episodic, fragmented, and without drama. Goldstein writes that the telling of these stories goes against academic rationalist tradition, a theory that supernatural belief declines with education and access to technology. Similarly, in her research on spirits in early modern Europe, Edwards writes that "widely held throughout Europe, belief in ghosts endured and even strengthened despite intellectual, cultural, and social changes in that period." Haunting stories do not adhere to the elitist idea that only those without education would believe in the supernatural. Tell a ghost story at any party, Goldstein says, and eventually someone will counter with their own personal haunting tale.

I took an ethnography course with Goldstein and I've interviewed her in my journalistic work. I have learned a lot about belief from her and from her research. She once described herself to me as an extreme cultural relativist, meaning that she aims to understand beliefs and their accompanying behaviour without judgment. I could never achieve this level of objectivity—she was researching infanticide at the time that she told me this—but I have tried to apply this gentle approach to supernatural beliefs since, however far removed they might be from my own.

In an article on the usefulness of ghost stories, folklorist Jeanie Banks Thomas writes that her students always want her to say, definitively, whether she believes that ghosts are real or not. She never responds. She tells them that the veracity of haunting experience narratives is of no interest to the folklore scholar. "To have scientific evidence for the supernatural, the existence of ghosts, and life beyond death would answer some of the most enduring questions of human existence," Thomas writes. "Folklore research, like other forms of scholarship, cannot sate that desire." Instead, folklorists analyze the story, looking for clues to better understand the society, culture, or person telling the tale. It's up to the storyteller to believe or doubt their experience.

The mother in the park had humiliated me by challenging my story and refusing to accept the possibility that it was true, but she'd also rattled me in a different way. My haunting is part of my family folklore. The hovering scribble sits on the same shelf in my memory as Martha, my imaginary friend, the pink flower girl dress I wore to my oldest sister's wedding, and stories about our badly behaved family dog. Some of these things are real and others might be imagined, but I had never thought to question their differences because together they told a story of who I was and who I would become.

*

I wrote to Walter to ask him if he recalled anything about the small bedroom. I worried that this request might seem strange. For this reason, I kept the details brief. I didn't describe the apparition to him, or call it a ghost, or tell him about my drawing. I referred to my issues as "nightmares" and mentioned that people believed the room was haunted. Walter was unfazed, however, and got back to me within a day. No, it hadn't been his daughter, he wrote, but his son, Matthew, who'd had unsettling dreams while sleeping in the little room. "He remembers the nightmares and some sort of hovering thing above him," Walter wrote. "He'd be around your age."

I reimagined my drawing, altered to feature a small boy in the bed with a black scribble above where he lay. The little boy had dark hair, wore striped pyjamas, held a bear. Walter encouraged me to contact Matthew, so I emailed him a list of six questions about the ghost. I hoped this wasn't stirring up unwelcome memories for him but my curiosity overrode my concern. A few days later I heard back. Matthew said he felt he'd been visited by a ghost in the little bedroom and that there had been "some type of floating apparition above my bed." I asked if his overall experience in Flavigny influenced any of the directions he took in adulthood. "No," he wrote. "I would not think that it did."

His answers were brief but I did not press him further. It was as if I'd asked him to recall a childhood bully we'd both encountered, and while I'd remained haunted by the experience Matthew had moved on. His response felt vindicating, though, as his memory was similar to my own. The details were not exact, but they were close. If I were mounting a case I'd bring him in as a witness. Did this prove anything? I wasn't certain. Like my mother, I didn't rule it out.

Sometimes I think my parents did me a disservice by normalizing supernatural beliefs, the earliest of which was my childhood ghost. The people in their orbit accepted and, as my mother said, even celebrated the possibility of spectral beings, but the ones in mine occasionally saw this kind of conviction as a threat. It is difficult to try to live in both worlds and not let one bleed into the other. Maybe this is why I studied folklore—serious scholarly work could legitimize my beliefs.

∗

My son is seven now, and, based on the results of the studies on childhood belief, he is on the cusp of discerning what is real from what is imaginary. He has a year of magical thinking left, maybe less. Just this morning I sat sandwiched on the couch between my children and my son showed me a pencil drawing of a dragon that he'd made in his sketchbook. I'd mistaken it for a snake, and at first he'd been bothered that I hadn't correctly identified his drawing. He brightened, however, when I said that dragons and snakes are in the same family, that they are both reptiles, and therefore look alike. My daughter, who is eleven now, elbowed me in the ribs, tilted her head, and gave me a hard stare. She wanted me to say that dragons weren't real, but I wouldn't. Not yet.

The research paper "Dragons and Dinosaurs: The Child's Capacity to Differentiate Fantasy from Reality" was published in the journal Child Development in 1979, the same year our family lived in Flavigny. The study centred on children from kindergarten and grades two, four, and six. Each child was given set of twenty cards featuring a figure that could be classified as fantastical or real.

The researchers, Patricia Morison and Howard Gardner, found that a child's ability to classify fantasy figures and to give an explanation for their choice increased with age. The older the child the more likely they were to employ logic, reasoning, and memory in discerning the real from the imaginary. Morison and Gardner concluded that young children believed in everything—magical and real—and that the fantastical aspects of their worlds slowly eroded as they learned each piece that was untrue. In their conclusion they write, "It may be that young children initially attribute reality status indiscriminately and that a category of unreal elements only gradually begins to form, leaving as an undifferentiated whole the larger category of reality."

The paper does not offer information about the sequence of this disintegration. I lost my ghost and my imaginary friend, Martha, after we returned home to Canada, but I can't remember in which order my other beliefs fell. Were fairies extinguished before or after dragons? Who went first, Santa Claus or the Easter Bunny? I was nearly eight when I gave up trying to fly, but I'd grown suspicious of the Tooth Fairy long before this. The crumbling of childhood memories and beliefs reminds me of a picture book by Julia Donaldson called The Paper Dolls, a story I often read with my children. In it, a little girl's mother helps her to make a string of paper dolls and the child imagines make-believe lands in which the paper dolls overcome various adversaries like a crocodile, a tiger, and a dinosaur, until one day they encounter a remorseless little boy who snips them into tiny pieces. The dolls are irreparable but they do not disappear. Instead, they reform and fly into the little girl's memory, which is a magical land of white mice and fireworks and a kind granny and all the lost items of childhood that are both real and imagined. I've read this book aloud more than any other in my life, and my voice wavers every time I get to the part about the little girl's memory. It feels familiar and welcoming, as if it was a place I visited often but had not returned to in a long time.

∗

The last time I visited the house in Flavigny I was in my twenties. I stayed there alone for several weeks while working on a screenplay. At night, I slept in the master bedroom that had been my parents' room when I was young. As they had in the past, the village streetlights went out every evening, although they did so at a later time now. I dreaded the switch from light to dark and would try to fall asleep early to avoid experiencing this. I mostly succeeded, but sometimes I woke late in the night and was unable to return to sleep. As I lay in the pitch black I occasionally thought about the ghost, wondering if it still appeared in the small room across the hall and if it was capable of materializing in the master bedroom. Would it remember me the same way I remembered it? This spooked me, but something different prevented me from sleeping. I'd been working as a reporter in Kyiv for the previous nine months and would return home at the end of my sojourn in Flavigny. I'd learned passable

Russian and Ukrainian phrases, had conquered the city's warren of underground streets, and at work I'd covered nightclub openings, art shows, and rock concerts and interviewed diplomats, politicians, and, once, an evangelical preacher some likened to a cult leader. I sensed that life back in Canada might not be as interesting. I didn't have any plans beyond these weeks in France and I was running out of money. I had no job prospects. I was heartsick, too, and this was affecting my ability to concentrate on writing. I feared that I would never finish the screenplay, and, if I did, that it wouldn't be any good. Life felt on the precipice of getting worse rather than better. This kind of sleepless fretting was somewhat new to me then, but I recognize it now as the midnight dread of adulthood—the mundane and profound life worries that are exacerbated in the late hours. A haunting, to be sure, but one of a different nature. The Something's the Matter never visited during the nights I spent alone in Flavigny. I'd grown out of my ghost, or, maybe, finding my adult mind dulled by reality, it had grown out of me.

*

I still tell my children the story of Something's the Matter. Once, I asked my son why it didn't frighten him as it had the other boy in the park. He said that I told it in a funny way and so he didn't find it scary. Also, he added, "it's not real." We were standing at the kitchen counter. I was chopping beets for borscht, a recipe I'd learned while living in Ukraine. My hands were blood red.

My son was peeling carrots. He'd grown over the last year and he no longer needed a stool to reach the counter and help prepare dinner. He was quiet for some time, peeling the carrot skins off in long curls. Then, he stopped for a moment and faced me.

"I felt sorry for you."

"You felt sorry for me as a child?"

"Yes, when you were little."

"But why?"

"Because that ghost was scaring you at night."

*

Recently I came across a painting of my father's showing two early twentieth-century figures cutting a path through a foreboding landscape. The men are photocopied images of Jack and Jim, the embalmers who'd worked at the funeral parlour when my father was young. To their right is a clear-cut forest and in the foreground, a thicket of yellowed and leafless trees casting green shadows. The painting has many ominous features, but one stands out as familiar to me: A red fog seeps in from the top right corner, hovering above the woods. The work was completed in 1999 and my father titled it "Jack and Jim and Something's the Matter." I have a vague memory of my father incorporating my childhood haunting into his art, but I hadn't seen this painting before. My father died that year so I couldn't ask him about the work. I'll never know if the title refers to the overall mood of the painting, a problem between the two embalmers, the clear-cut, or, as I saw it, the shapeless red fog. As with the presence in the small bedroom, so many of the questions I have about the painting will remain unanswered.

*

Today, the house in Flavigny belongs to Virgil and Anne's oldest daughter, Maud, a medievalist who works as a professor of English at Haverford College in Pennsylvania. She spends every summer in France and plans to relocate to the home permanently after she retires. When I wrote to her and asked about the haunted bedroom, she recounted the same story that my mother told me about Virgil sleeping on the floor after sensing the sinister cold. Maud slept in that room with her younger sister, Melissa, until she was eight and moved to the attic. They both had occasional nightmares, but nothing that could be described as an apparition. Maud did tell me stories of other children who'd been woken by night terrors in the small room since I'd slept there, including a little blond boy named Noah, the son of a painter who'd spent time at the house, as well as Maud's goddaughter Molly. The stories she relayed were like most haunting experience narratives, fragmented, and without a beginning, middle, or end. As with other ghost stories, Maud offered grounding details. She is the person who told me that the little bedroom was an extension built in the nineteenth century, and she reminded me of the window that looked over the garden and also that the headboard had been tall. She sent me a photograph of my former bed, taken recently, with two tiny kittens tangled in its sheets. I took all of these elements, images and words, and incorporated them into my own story along with the memories I have from spending time in Flavigny as a child and also as an adult. I added Matthew's story, succinct, but valuable in its echo of my own. I gathered my mother's memories, and the images from my father's painting. I took what had been passed on from Virgil and Anne and filed these details as well. All together these form a pastiche that will change and grow each time I retell the story of the Something's the Matter.

Maud's own two children never slept in the little bedroom. Partly because her mother, Anne, had taken it over by then. But also, she wrote, "I didn't want them to." Finally, Maud recalled my experience, as relayed by my mother. She remembered what I'd named the apparition, and also that I'd made a drawing of a little girl with yellow hair lying in a bed with a great black scribble hovering above her. "Of all the childhood hauntings that happened in that room over the years," Maud wrote, "I remember your experience as the definitive one."

*

There will always be unknowable shapes in our physical and spiritual landscapes, ones that we will return to and worry over and that will humble us with their mystery. The story of the inky blackness above my childhood bed, as with all personal haunting narratives, is up to the listener to decipher. The person telling the story is the authority on its veracity but the listener is free to choose how they react, what they believe, what to take and what to leave behind. Piaget told us that we create our world, our understanding tweaked by applying logic and memory to each new experience. My interpretation is that matter forms our physical world, but stories shape the rest.

Lessons for Female Success

LESSON ONE: *By horrible example, a woman learns how not to get killed.*

I am a teenager, working at a summer camp near Huntsville, Ontario. It is the mid-nineties and I am wearing an orange and green tie-dye Grateful Dead t-shirt and my hair is waist-length and bleached by the sun. It is early in the season and the staff are readying the grounds for when the campers will arrive. Today, I am tasked with searching every cabin on camp for the name of the vilest sexual predator that my country has seen so that I can sand it away. These were the marks he left behind when he worked as a camp counsellor here, about fifteen years earlier. The camp director has decided not to erase the rapist's name from the official records of previous campers and staff that hang on plaques along the interior walls of the dining hall, but he does not want anyone seeking out this criminal's teenage scrawl with their flashlights at night—the signature of a man who has recently been convicted of sexually assaulting, torturing, and murdering a series of girls around my age. The graffitied cabin walls are a silent roll call of everyone who has drifted through this place over the past few decades. It can be difficult to decipher one name from another, so I learn to recognize this man's handwriting, the round looped vowels in his name, the slant of the consonants. I must divine the locations of his signatures and learn to identify his preferred tools: on a windowsill in thick black marker; on a bunk ladder in ballpoint pen. I look for patterns to emerge but there are none. It takes an entire day to sand his name from the walls, rafters, and ceilings of the cabins, and still, I can't be sure I've found every one.

There is an old European ballad about a woman who outwits a murderer. He had disguised himself as a knight, wooing her with a magic song she could not refuse. She wore a dress and rode her best mare into the woods to be with him, although her father had warned against this. He had told her that no one who goes that way ever comes back. She found the knight deep in the forest and together they rode to the seashore. Once there, he revealed a gallows on which there hung seven women. He gave her a choice between dying by hanging and dying by sword. She opted for the sword, but asked that he remove his coat first. "A maid's blood spurts a great way and it would be a pity to splatter you," she told him. He looked down to unbutton his coat and in one fluid movement she stole his sword and sliced off his head.

This is one of 305 songs collectively known as the Child ballads, sung poems rooted in the oral tradition of the British Isles and dating back to the fifteenth century. Just as we associate fairy tales with the Brothers Grimm, these ballads are named for their collector, nineteenth-century Harvard English professor and folklorist Francis James Child. He was the first to address these folk songs with a scholarly eye and he organized them into five published volumes, assigning each ballad a number to facilitate future study. I first encountered them in graduate school and was immediately taken by their imagery and gory drama. The action in these tales is present-tense and immediate, the past a vague and unmentioned country. The stories focus on a central event and begin at the height of the tension—an incident that is, almost always, sexually violent. These are sorrowful songs where women are raped, punished to death for loving the wrong man, abducted by vicious relatives and strangers, and burned at the stake for affairs of the heart. The narrator never editorializes; she offers the story but no analysis or comment. The ballad about the murderer and the maiden is Child Ballad 4, and is called "Lady Isobel and the Elf Knight." It is unusual among the others in the canon because the woman escapes.

LESSON TWO: *For a woman, stepping outside her house is dangerous..*

It is mid-morning and I am lying on the pink fold-out couch I have used as a bed since moving to Ukraine six months earlier for a job with the *Kyiv Post* newspaper. I am in my late twenties. I can occasionally see a crow swoop by the window; I know they perch on the branches of the poplar trees in the courtyard of our apartment complex. I hadn't closed my curtains the night before because I was afraid of what could lurk in the space between the folds of the drapery and the windowpane. In the darkness, it had seemed as if it could hold a body. My bedroom door is slightly ajar and I can hear my roommate, Tamara, speaking in a low voice with our landlord, Ihor. He has come to change the locks because my keys were in a purse that two men stole from me last night. I'd been on my way home from a party when this happened. It was past midnight. The light in the archway that leads to our apartment block was out although this was not unusual. People often stole the lightbulb and weeks would pass before it was replaced. As I entered the courtyard, a young man appeared from my left. He wore a black leather jacket and a black wool cap, and he spoke with urgency. I could not understand him. I know words and phrases in Russian and Ukrainian but my comprehension is limited. The man's behaviour was strange. Men, for the most part, do not bother me in Kyiv. If they pay special attention or look at me, it is because I am a foreigner, dressed in American clothes. I am a curiosity, but never an object of desire or harassment.

This man was different. He wanted something from me and he looked desperate.

He took my hand in a strong and painful grip. I pulled away, hard, and freed myself. The white mitten that I'd been wearing fell to the ground. I felt a rush of air, as if a sudden gust of wind had blown from the shadows behind me. I turned slightly to see a blur of movement. It was a second man running towards me from an opposite shadowy corner than the first. I wondered if I had been screaming and if the man was coming to my rescue. He was not. He threw me to the ground with a full-body slam. My tailbone bore the initial impact of my fall. Then, the back of my skull hit the pavement. I heard a high-pitched ringing in my ears. I struggled, kicked, and bit, but the men overpowered me. I had two thoughts in quick succession: First, I thought I might die. Second, I thought, No, my voice will save me. By then I could hear myself screaming. I didn't know if I was using words in English or Ukrainian or Russian or if I was shrieking into the abyss. I thought I was saying, "No, no, no." I might have been asking, "Why?"

One man covered my mouth. I screeched through his fingers, tasting the salty sweat of his palm. I was dragged further back into the archway, away from the street. I continued to yell. The men turned me over onto my stomach and I felt my purse being lifted up over my head. Lying still, I realized that I was alone again. In the darkness the two men disappeared immediately from view, but I could hear the crunch of their footsteps across the snowy courtyard, receding into the night.

Now, this morning, there is the sound of Ihor sighing as he works on our front door, and the occasional buzz of his electric drill fastening the new lock into place. Ihor telephones our apartment every week and relays messages through Tamara, who is the only roommate who speaks Ukrainian. He calls to tell us that he is worried for our safety. He asks us not to speak English in the hallways of the building and not to walk alone after dark. He wants to know that we've been locking our doors. He suggests, frequently, that we should return home. You are nice girls, he tells Tamara during these phone calls. You should go home to Canada. Now, his fear has come to pass and one of us has been harmed despite his many warnings.

I was nearly thirty when I encountered the Child ballads in my first year of graduate school. At the time, I was single and living on my own. On weeknights, I'd time my dinner so that I could eat while watching the procedural crime drama *Law and Order: Special Victims Unit*. It was a spinoff from the original network show and featured sexually violent crimes, largely against women, although sometimes the victims were children or members of other vulnerable groups. The lead detective, Olivia Benson, played by Mariska Hargitay, was exactly the person you'd want to encounter after surviving an assault—her kind-eyed look of consternation conveying that you are safe and that she understands the gravity of what has happened to you. She treats every victim with the same respect, no matter if they are gambling addicts or sex workers,

Russian mail-order brides or wealthy heiresses. She is particularly kind to children. She is a listener, a helper. I'd been a fan of the show for years, but had started this ritualistic watching after moving to Newfoundland to begin a master's degree in folklore.

One Wednesday night a month I'd miss watching SVU because I worked the door at Folk Night, a live music event at the Ship Pub in downtown St. John's. I took the cover charge and handed out raffle tickets. It was a volunteer job and I got paid in beer. I was learning about the Child ballads in my classes, but on Folk Night I could hear them performed during the open mic portion of the evening. Sometimes there was a duo—I remember a pair of brothers from Bell Island with an extensive ballad repertoire—but more often the singers performed solo. The songs were sorrowful, and, particularly in women's voices, they sounded like a keen, a sung lament. They were mostly about romance, although this seemed to be a veneer for violence, rape, and murder, often at the hands of a woman's close family member, as in Child Ballad 233, "Mill o Tifty's Annie." In this story a miller's daughter named Annie falls in love with Andrew Lammie, a trumpeter for a local lord, but her parents feel he is beneath her because he is poor. In some versions her father is convinced she's been bewitched by Andrew Lammie's music. Both parents beat Annie in an attempt to change her mind, but it's her brother who breaks her back and kills her.

The Folk Night crowd listened quietly to the ballads. They didn't speak over the singers as people did with live performances on other nights. The balladeers didn't have accompanying instruments or a band, just their voice, so they could be quickly overpowered by a talkative audience. The audience understood that a ballad isn't background music, it's a story. If you don't pay attention, you'll miss what it's telling you.

I enjoyed those nights at the Ship. I liked the smell of wet coats and stale beer and the dimmed lighting. I liked the records that lined the pub walls displaying the names of bands that I'd never heard of, like Lady Luck, or the Saddle Sores. I liked interacting with the patrons at the door, answering their questions, and waiving the cover charge for the musicians. I also relished the quiet times later in the night when I'd sit on my high stool with a bottle of beer in my hand, listening to ballads where one woman after another met a violent end. I have never been a singer. I didn't know how you could remember the tunes and all the words to these songs. It seemed like magic. At the close of the evening, after I'd cashed out and handed the night's revenue to the bartender, I'd walk home alone with my keys arranged between the fingers of my closed fist. This way, I might have a chance of fighting back if I was attacked in the dark streets.

LESSON THREE: *A woman's resources for protection are slim.*

He was wearing a balaclava, or he was wearing a leather gimp mask that zipped up the front of his face. He wore his shorts around his ankles, or he pulled them aside, or he'd been wearing pants but had removed them. The doorway, where he stood waiting for us, was backlit, or it was spotlit from above. He'd brushed past us as we left the bar in Toronto's west end. I think our shoulders touched. I think he stopped to grab one of those free entertainment magazines from a bin at the curb. Or that had been a different person, an innocent bystander who'd unknowingly wandered into the narrative that would become my police report. Maybe this passerby was a lucky decoy as the man readied himself in the doorway, or maybe he was an unexpected annoyance as he waited for me and my friend and former roommate Tamara. He knew we'd be walking by, which means he must have been in the bar with us that afternoon as it slid into early evening. He needed to wait out the man who joined our table and wouldn't leave because he wanted to tell Tamara that she looked so much like an actor from Coronation Street. That man was still there when we left, so I don't think he was the flasher. It was impossible to identify the flasher by his face mask (which was leather or wool) or by his exposed penis (from dropped shorts or baggy ones pulled to the side), so maybe it was the man who'd harassed us in the pub. We hurried away from him, and, on a parallel road, tried to flag down a passing police car to report the incident, but the officers stared blankly at us as they drove by.

A few weeks later, there are two young police officers parked near the same bar when I walk by with Tamara and a second friend, Rachel. We've just told Rachel the story of that night and, seeing the police car, she urges us to report it.

The two officers seem distracted. Maybe they are in the middle of some other case and we've interrupted them. They do not get out of their car so we lean down and tell our story through their open window.

"It happened two weeks ago?"

"We tried to flag down a police car to say something, but they wouldn't stop," Tamara says.

"Yeah, well, at that time of night people always try to get rides home," the officer says. "That's not our responsibility."

"We weren't trying to get a ride home," Tamara tells them. "We were trying to tell them that a man was exposing himself to women leaving the pub."

"So, what?" the officer in the passenger seat asks. "Are you scarred for life?"

No one knows what to say. The experience with the flasher was unsettling, but I am still able to sleep at night. Is this what he means?

One officer smirks and the other one rolls his eyes. Then, they wave us off.

Ballads are survivors and they have travelled a long distance. The ancient songs warbled across centuries, passing from one singer to the next, wending through the countryside and in and out of towns, and eventually the sung poems crossed the Atlantic on sailing ships, tucked into the repertoires of the European emigrants on board. A few of the Child ballads take place at sea. In "Bonnie Annie," a merchant's daughter falls in love with a ship captain. He takes her on board but a problem arises and the sailors believe Annie is the cause of this bad luck. She offers to throw herself overboard and all the men agree that this is the best solution. Afterwards, the captain fishes her dead body from the water and gives her a proper land burial. I imagine "Bonnie Annie" being sung in the cramped quarters of an immigrant ship and how a young woman listening might relate to the merchant's daughter. She could conjure the sea in Annie's voyage, the boundless water, the darkness of its depths. The story might be more powerful for the listener who can draw on concrete images, although knowing the terrain isn't necessary with balladry. The narratives are told without context or identifying details so the story takes place in the landscape of the listeners' minds. It is for this reason that the songs adapted so well to the deep brush, to the endless whiteness of snow, to the mountains, and to the rocky island in the middle of the North Atlantic where I first heard them.

I learned about the serial rapist and his crimes the summer before I'd had to scrub his name from the cabin walls, when my mother visited on my day off from camp. We sat in a small-town laundromat watching the dryer tumble my clothes and she told me how her friend, an editor at a national newspaper, was seeing veteran trial reporters, men grizzled and hardened from working the crime beat, return to the newsroom and weep. My mother said she couldn't tell me any names, or what she knew, only that it was terrible and that I should be careful. But how could I avoid being raped and killed? It seemed a matter of luck and circumstance, not something one could evade.

Some of the women in the ballads attempt to outrun their pursuer, but the process is harrowing and often requires supernatural strength and ability. I can only take this to mean that the goal is nearly always impossible. In Child Ballad 22, "The Two Magicians," a blacksmith threatens to take a young woman's virginity and so begins a long and magical chase. She eludes him by transforming into a rose, but he then becomes a bee, so she tries again, this time turning into a fish, but the blacksmith becomes an angler and reels her in with his rod. She becomes a star and he a cloud that shrouds her light. She becomes a rabbit and he a greyhound that pursues her. She dies and he becomes the earth she's interred in. By the ballad's end the blacksmith exhausts the young woman and she gives in to him. I've read that versions exist where the woman manages to get away. I've yet to hear one, but I haven't given up on the possibility.

The day after my attack in Kyiv I spend three hours in the Department of Hooligan Affairs at the police station near the office building where I work. A pubescent-looking officer refers to my assailants as devils, more than once, while we look at hundreds of black-and-white mug shots on a computer screen. Any one of these men could have been one of the culprits, but to me, they all look like different versions of the same white man. I sometimes make a motion to stop the process and re-evaluate one photo or another, but I know this is futile.

The officer's shoulders slump as we near the end. I feel a vague guilt for not finding the wanted men. He had seemed so hopeful for a match, although I'm not sure why. A woman attacked in the night, a stolen purse, it must happen all the time. The devils remain at large.

As I alternated between watching episodes of SVU and listening to ballads at Folk Night these two narrative forms grew increasingly close to one another, sometimes overlapping in plot. In SVU's tenth season a woman unknowingly marries her rapist in an episode called "Trials." The plot twist is revealed just before the credits roll, leaving the audience to imagine what she will do with this newfound information. This episode carries an echo of Child Ballad 5, "Gil Brenton," in which a woman is raped by a masked man in the woods who ultimately turns out to be the lord she marries. The premise in both the television show and the ballad is outrageous and implausible, but the advice that might be gleaned from each is universal: Trust your instincts; question everything; don't get comfortable; if something seems off, then it probably is; not everyone is who they seem. It is a paranoid way to view the world but it is also pragmatic.

The ballads are likewise cautionary tales. In Wishful Willful Wily Women: Lessons for Female Success in the Child

Ballads, folklorist Polly Stewart analyzed the repertoire of female ballad singers—North American women who learned these sung poems via their settler-ancestors—and she noticed that there were messages in the songs the female singers chose to perform. The stories within the ballads acted as warnings for the younger women in the audience. The singers' lessons were coded, but clear: "For a woman, stepping outside the house is a dangerous act," Stewart writes, and "a woman's resources for protecting herself are slim." Finally, "by horrible example, a woman learns how not to get killed."

This paper was assigned reading for the course I took on balladry, and I'd expected it to be heavy, possibly boring. Instead, I connected with Stewart's lessons. I felt that I'd lived a distilled version of them already. Some situations had merely been uncomfortable and others were terrifying, but all were, in some way, unsafe. The ballads, like the procedural crime drama, allowed me a space to process some of these events, to explore fear, rage, and powerlessness while also remaining in control.

After the officers dismiss us, Rachel, Tamara, and I decide to try and report the flasher a second time. We walk to the nearest police station, and, while we are there, we relay how the officers responded to our initial attempt to tell the story. We are given two forms to complete—one for our complaint about the officers and another to report the incident from two weeks before. The next week, I begin a new job at a small non-profit organization and on the first morning a female detective visits my office to question me about the exhibitionist. My new co-workers watch with interest as I greet the police officer and we step into the hall to speak. After work, I call Tamara to compare notes. She'd seen a leather mask while I'd seen a balaclava. She'd seen shorts around his ankles while I'd seen them pulled to the side. I remember a man brushing swiftly by my shoulder, but he isn't part of Tamara's storyline. The details in our accounts were different, and yet the core of both narratives was exactly the same.

Later that week, a second officer calls me at my workplace. He is a superior to the officer who'd rebuffed our initial attempts to tell him about the incident. He is warm, and he lets me know he's on my side. He tells me that no one should be chastised for reporting a crime. He agrees it was inappropriate for the officer to ask if we'd been "scarred for life."

"But, I mean, now what?" he asks, in his gentle, even tone. "The officer is sorry, and he won't do this again. He's been reprimanded. But what do you want me to do?"

I don't know what to say. He interrupts my silence.

"I guess what I'm asking is, do you want him to apologize to you in person, or in writing, or what? Do you want this man to lose his job? He's got a family, but, you know, if that's what you want."

The officer is exaggerating. We both understand that I will not demand that the man lose his job. I will not destruct his life and family, nor do I have the power to do so. It's unclear why he offers this, except perhaps to show me that everything about this situation, including my complaint, is ridiculous. Or perhaps he is teasing me. I laugh a lot when I speak. It's how I communicate and I mostly don't dwell on this. Sometimes, though, I wonder if it makes people think I am not a serious person. Or that I don't warrant gravity. Maybe this is what is happening with the officer and his bizarre suggestion.

He remains silent, waiting for my response.

"No, of course not," I tell him. "I just don't want him to say that kind of thing again."

I spent nearly seven years in graduate school, having continued on to a PhD after finishing my master's degree. Around the time I was writing my doctoral thesis, a friend posted on social media saying she would no longer watch television or film that featured violence against women, where a woman's rape or death was part of the plot. She mentioned SVU in particular. There were think pieces being published at the time that echoed this friend's position and I wondered if I should stop consuming this type of media as well. I was married by then, and I had a new baby. I didn't go out at night anymore, and I hardly ever walked home alone in the dark. I'd had to quit my volunteer job at Folk Night because it was impossible to fit into my new life. I still watched SVU, although not in the habitual way I'd done in the past. Sometimes in the late hours when the baby woke me and I couldn't fall back to sleep, I'd turn on the television and catch a rerun. I found the show just as riveting as I had before, although I was beginning to age out of their audience demographic. This isn't a problem for the franchise. There were always going to be young women to take my place—both as viewers and as the victims onscreen. SVU would carry on and ultimately earn the title of longest-running prime-time drama in the history of television.

I understood the problem of depicting women's trauma in film and television, but I wasn't sure this applied to SVU, which was its own particular kind of fantasy where victims of sexual violence were treated with dignity and seriousness by the police they encountered. For me, this was the crux of the problem. I had believed an exchange with law enforcement would be similar to what I'd seen on the show. I imagined that I'd go to a downtown station with a problem and meet Detective Olivia Benson there. She would look at me with her nut-brown eyes, absorb my fear, listen to my story, and tell me what to do next.

On the late nights I came across SVU reruns I always watched until the story wrapped up—satisfied only when the perp was revealed, caught, and justly punished. It might not be how the process looks in reality, but it is something to strive for. There is a lesson in that, too.

In an email exchange nearly fifteen years later, I ask Rachel what she recalls from the night we encountered the police officers. Her memories are fairly similar to mine, except for a crucial part of the story I'd forgotten. Around the same time the man had followed me and Tamara from the bar and exposed himself, there had been a string of nearby assaults—one woman had been stalked home and attacked on her front lawn, another had been kidnapped and assaulted over the course of a week.

"That's why I thought it was important to report the flasher," she wrote.

In 2004 there were 2,723 sexual assaults in Toronto—a number that includes the masked man who followed me and Tamara from a bar and exposed himself in a lit doorway. Exhibitionists tend to escalate to more dangerous, sexually deviant behaviour, but it's impossible to know if the man we encountered went on to commit further crimes.

There is a poetic phrase in ballads that is used as a prelude to an act of violence, but one that is disguised as a romantic gesture: "He takes her by her lily-white hand." When I hear this or read it on the page, rather than a seventeenth-century maid and knight, I see myself in a dark archway with a shadowy man in a black cap. I see him take my hand, and I see myself pulling away, my white woollen mitten drifting slowly to the ground as if it were a feather. I can then imagine one of my roommates, Shanon, coming home an hour or so later and spotting the single mitt—its whiteness standing out on concrete path—and knowing it was mine, and how a terrible feeling had come over her at the sight of it lying there, strangely out of place. How the feeling grew when she found our front door locked, the apartment dark and empty. How quickly she picked up the telephone when I called a few minutes after she arrived home. I'd been phoning our home repeatedly from a nearby hookah café, where I was being comforted by the night cleaning staff, a quartet of babushkas who let me inside when I appeared at the door, the shoulder of my peacoat ripped off, wearing one mitt, my apartment keys and wallet stolen. As it looked increasingly like I had nowhere to go, one golden-toothed baba had offered to take me home with her. She struggled to communicate with me, as I understood so little of the language. She came to my side and gently tugged the ripped shoulder of my coat back into place, and said, "No. Men." It was her way of assuring me I would be safe at her home. There were no men living there.

Shanon came for me before I left with the kind baba. At home, I noticed my missing mitten lying on a table in the hall and I dropped the other by its side. Reunited, they were a lily-white pair once more. I couldn't stand what they'd come to symbolize, though, so I threw them away the next morning.

I left Kyiv in spring when the cherry blossoms were beginning to flower. From the back seat of the airport taxi, I noticed how the white petals were made nearly transparent by the morning sun. It had been grey that winter, without texture, or definition, without clouds. The trees and buildings were casting shadows I'd never seen before, or maybe that I hadn't noticed, and I had the thought that I was leaving too soon. The city was going to reveal itself in the next few months and I would not be there.

I never saw my attackers again but they have returned to me, unbidden, in the years since. They appear when I rise too quickly from a hard-seated chair, sending a shot of pain up my back. Each time I was pregnant they were my phantom companions, walking step by step with me as my injured tailbone creaked under my heft and sway. I pass them, still, in the shadows of dusk when I walk home from the library at night, and sometimes I can hear their footsteps, growing fainter, pitter-pattering into the darkness.

The SVU stories are often inspired by real events, including one episode that hews closely to the case of the serial killer and rapist who'd worked at my summer camp. Similarly, some of the ballads are based on true stories. The young woman beaten by her family and ultimately murdered by her brother in "Tifty's Annie" is said to be based on the honour killing of Agnes Smith of Fyvie, Scotland. She'd lived with her family at the Mill of Tifty near the castle of Fyvie, which is presumably how she crossed paths with the lord's trumpeter. She died on January 19, 1673, and is buried in a local graveyard. Her headstone has the ballad's title inscribed below her name. It has been upkept, repaired, and most recently replaced with a polished granite cross that towers above the other graves. Over centuries, in stone and in song, Annie's story persists.

I spend the day looking for and then erasing the murderer's signature and this is more emotional and laborious than I expect. The last name I remove is over the bunk where I sleep, and, before erasing it, I have a friend take my portrait underneath his signature, me gesturing upwards with one hand, steadying myself on a rafter with the other. I want to record this act of revision. Not for him, but for the women and girls he raped, murdered, and disappeared, and for me, so I can remember this day. Then, I scour the wall clean.

Years from now, in the intangible space of the internet, a place my younger self could never have imagined, someone will post an anonymous message on Reddit about that day.

"I worked at a summer camp that [   ] used to work at. It's tradition to always sign your bunk, so his name was all over the cabins. Since most Canadians know the story, the camp had to go and try to find each of his signatures and sanded them all down to not remind the campers and counsellors that he used to sleep where they were sleeping."

This small paragraph reads like a legend. As if the tale were a frightening campfire story about a tragedy that took place in the past, complete with unthinkable acts of violence and a lingering bogeyman who haunts each new generation, lurking in the memories of the cabin walls. I will search for myself in this paragraph, but I won't find any hint of the day I spent sanding the monster's scrawl. I am nowhere, but despite my effort to erase his marks, he is everywhere. He has scarred for life.

Chimera

IN MESOPOTAMIA, PREGNANT WOMEN WORE amulets in the shape of a feathery, lion-headed demon called Lamashtu. She was known as "she who erases" because she could make a fetus, infant, or sometimes even a new mother, disappear. In the past, Romanian women wore tiny books on strings around their necks, each page a handwritten incantation against Samca, the beast who devours the unborn. Devout Catholics pray to the image of St. Catherine of Sweden, patron saint of miscarriage, that she might keep their child safe in the womb. And me? I had no prayer, spell, or incantation. Instead, I wrote down a diagnosis I was hoping against, once in English, a second time in Italian, and then folded the paper into my wallet.

*

The first person I told about my pregnancy was a stranger. She was a Polish traveller named Masha and we met at the pension where we were both staying in Alghero, a town on the Italian island of Sardinia. She'd been sailing the

Mediterranean and this was her last port of call. I was on a weekend visit, escaping the student dorm where I lived that summer just outside of London. On our final night, we dined together at a café along the sea wall. That was thirteen years ago but the details of the evening remain clear, like how the setting sun turned the light orange, the sound of the waves beneath the restaurant's terrace, and how we'd become lost in the narrow, winding streets on our way home. I remember the minutiae of that night because it's a plot point in a story I write every year, usually around the time summer's hazy edges slip into the sharpness of fall. In some versions, like this one, I begin with meeting Masha and in others she doesn't appear at all. If pressed, she might remember meeting me. It's somewhat unusual to encounter a solo woman traveller who also happens to be pregnant. If she does think of me, perhaps discovering the photograph we posed for over dinner, our wine glasses lifted high (mine filled with sparkling water) and the light-dappled sea behind us, she might briefly wonder and then calculate, as I have, on occasion, how old my child would be now. She might also question if there was ever any child at all. Because when I told her my secret the words hovered in the air between us like an apparition. Hearing it said out loud, and the unsure way I said it, made it sound like a lie, as if it were something I was fabricating to make myself seem more interesting.

I hardly believed it myself. I always said I'd never have children. And yet with the knowledge of impending parenthood, I'd begun to plan, moulding my existing life around a new shiny date in the future when everything would change. My daily patterns would shift, I'd need to reschedule major academic events like my comprehensive exams, I'd need to rearrange the furniture in the spare bedroom, which was my office, to accommodate a crib and a change table. It would require refitting my scholar's brain to include not one but two lives beyond my own.

These imagined plans would unfold back in St. John's, Newfoundland, where I lived with my relatively new partner, Andrew. We'd moved in together that spring and amidst boxes and chaos we'd parted for the summer. He went north to Labrador, where along with his fellow scientists he'd look for signs of climate change in shrubs of the Mealy Mountains. Around the same time, I boarded a plane to England. I was taking a field course as part of my graduate work in folklore. It was called The English Cultural Landscape and we explored the mythology, history, and material culture of this island and its people through a series of field trips that included the absurd collections of long-dead Victorians, the occasional castle, postwar suburbs, wattle and daub cottages, derelict factories, and council flats. There were a few older students, like me, but mostly they were twenty-year-olds on their first trip abroad. Before we left Canada I'd been assigned the task of teaching assistant and the department head asked if I could also act as a dorm manager. I'd declined. I didn't want to deal with the aftermath of boozy bar fights, lovelorn youth, or knocked-up undergrads. In my early thirties, a little too old to be on this extended, seven-week class trip, I was in one of the predicaments I'd hoped to avoid. A few days after arriving in England I'd discovered

I was pregnant, unceremoniously taking the test in the shared bathroom at my dorm.

The second line, the one that confirms the pregnancy, was faint. Compounding this confusing result was the fact that a few days later an ultrasound wasn't able to show anything in my womb. There was some kind of growth—it looked like a black stone or hole on the screen—but it wasn't fetus-shaped.

"It's still early, love," a kindly ultrasound technician told me during my appointment at the hospital near the dorm. The first doctor I visited had floated the possibility that the pregnancy might be ectopic, which is a potentially fatal condition where the fetus develops outside the womb, most commonly in the Fallopian tube. He based this theory on my hormone levels, which weren't doubling as expected, and on my medical history. Exploratory surgery had recently unearthed years of extensive scarring from endometriosis. "You're riddled with it" is how the surgeon put it when I came to in the operating theatre. The endometrial buildup increases the risk that the embryo will get stuck in the Fallopian tube. Based on my surgeon's findings and the British doctor's hunch, I wrote the words "ectopic pregnancy" on a small piece of paper that I kept in my wallet for an EMS attendant to discover if I fell unconscious from internal bleeding. Before leaving for Alghero, I wrote what I hoped was the Italian translation—encinto ectopica—on the back of the original note. I'd intended the information to act in the same way as a MedicAlert bracelet does, but the note became a sort of talisman, a charm against encroaching threat.

*

When I woke on my final morning in Alghero, Masha was gone and I'd started to bleed. On the flight back to London I tried to distract myself from what I assumed were the first stages of pregnancy loss by watching the Mediterranean landscape reveal itself from the vantage of the plane's oval window. The craggy yellow cliffs hugged the azure water. Inland, I could see the old town's maze of skinny streets and terracotta rooftops and the wall that wrapped around the city. Then, a wide swath of beach with its sunbathers roasting like turkeys under the midsummer Mediterranean sun. In that moment of take-off, a shaft of sunlight swept across my body and in its warmth I could nearly convince myself that life, both my own and the tiny orb of cells growing within me, would lift, rise, and stay on course.

A sudden pain interrupted my thoughts. It felt like an explosion inside my body. We reached cruising altitude and I crawled over my sleeping seatmate to vomit in the plane's sole toilet. I spent the rest of the flight in the bathroom, ignoring the steward repeatedly rapping on the door. Finally, I sat up in a sweat and buckled myself in for landing. At the airport pharmacy I looked for painkillers but I didn't know what might harm a growing fetus, if it was still growing. The ache in my side and the nausea were overwhelming and I asked a security guard for help. He showed me to a cot in a triage room at the end of a long hallway and quickly left, closing the door behind him. A woman wearing a fluorescent crossing-guard vest came

to see me and I explained that I was eight weeks pregnant. I told her that I was worried it might be ectopic. The
woman told me that the only thing she could do was call
an ambulance and that would be very expensive for me.

"Is that what you want?" she asked.

I was unsure. I told her I needed more time.

"Stay here for an hour," she said. "If I come back and
you're gone, then I'll know your decision."

Half an hour later, I took a bus back to the dorm,
clutching my side.

The next day I returned to the hospital where I'd had
my earlier tests. I met a pregnant teenager named Daisy
in the waiting room. I'd seen her there on my first visit.
She was wiry and small, and she already had one toddler.
Her mother was with her and read back issues of Hello
magazine while Daisy asked me questions. She wanted to
know when I was due, and if we might exchange email
addresses so we could meet up during our pregnancies
and after our babies were born. I explained that I'd be
returning to Canada in a few weeks.

"Let's keep in touch anyhow," she said. "Maybe our
babies will grow up to be pen pals." I found her optimism
touching, but I also found it sad.

Another week of blood-taking and ultrasounds followed.
I never saw the same physician twice because they worked
on a rotating schedule. One day I met with a beautiful
doctor with glossy black hair and red lips. She had an
upper-crust accent and made disparaging comments about
the working-class town we were in. She called it a hole and
said she couldn't wait to get back to London. I was outside

the British class system but she assumed we were on the same rung. I imagined she would not say the same things to Daisy. She clicked her tongue as she read over my file.

"You will have a big bleed," she said. "Then this will be all over."

She implied that the pregnancy, its loss, and my time in this cinder-block postwar town would be relegated to the same dusty corner of my memory. She was, in some ways, correct.

When I was not at the hospital I was on a tour bus, lurching across country roads. I always sat with the same woman, a mature student from Bell Island who had four grown boys.

"You remind me of a pregnant woman," she said one day, tilting her head and raising one eyebrow.

I shrugged, my eyes heavy-lidded from the movement of the bus, my head falling against the window. Every time I woke, at another abbey, factory, or Tudor home, it was with a full bladder and a sense of dread.

At the hospital I got to know a Scottish nurse who was kind and fierce and took a shine to me because of my Scots-Gaelic surname. She had soft brown curled hair and was about fifty years old. I can't remember her name, and yet, she probably saved my life.

"She is going to be on a flight home to Canada and we are going to lose track of her," the nurse said to the doctor on call on a Friday afternoon in early August, handing him my file. She believed the pretty doctor's diagnosis was incorrect, and that rather than an impending miscarriage I had an ectopic pregnancy. If not treated immediately, my tube would rupture. So many doctors had hemmed and hawed over the hormone results, the empty womb in repeated ultrasounds, but this nurse hollered.

The doctor phoned me at my dorm a few minutes later.

"Don't go anywhere this weekend and if you feel anything, I mean any hint of pain, come to the hospital immediately," he said. Then he instructed me to come in on Monday morning for surgery.

I called Andrew from a pay phone on the town's high street, a flow of Saturday morning shoppers streaming by on either side of the exposed booth. I used the emergency satellite telephone number and hoped he wouldn't panic when he was called to the phone by the person on duty. He told me he'd heard wolves howling the night before, a mournful sound that echoed along the mountain pass. I told him that he was a father, but, also, that he wasn't. He was quiet for a while afterwards, but we didn't have time for long silences. We couldn't afford them. I would have surgery. He would arrive in a week. We would keep our plans to see London and the west coast of Ireland.

I spent Sunday night at a local pub, drinking pints with an old friend who'd come to visit me from London. I needed to see someone familiar, someone who would let me drink beer while pregnant. It felt strange after being so careful—no coffee, no soft cheese, certainly no alcohol. I drank pint after pint and my friend didn't protest. She didn't say, *What if they're wrong and the baby is fine?* This was what I was both afraid of and hopeful for. We stayed until dark. I felt a twinge in my side and wondered if this was my baby—or at least the beginnings of a baby, which would soon be the end. I wondered if this feeling was the fetus growing, stretching my tube by the tiniest but most dangerous degrees. For every development towards life this being made, I inched closer to death.

I arrived at the hospital on Monday morning and the Scottish nurse met me with relief.

"I was so worried you'd gone," she said in her thick, comforting brogue. She showed me into a triage room where I changed into a hospital gown and placed my belongings in a plastic bag. She stuck an IV in my arm and handed me a stack of magazines. I sat there for three hours. At one point I overheard a distressed patient. "I'm in the middle of having a miscarriage," she said, then caught her breath and cried a little. "So I'm wondering if I still belong in the prenatal unit?"

She asked again, "Where do I belong?"

*

Eventually, I was given a bed in a public ward—yet another dorm—to wait for my surgery. I would need to spend the night but was not allowed to eat. I watched reruns of American sitcoms on the mini television attached to my bed. The next morning and afternoon passed slowly until, very suddenly, I was wheeled into the pre-op room. In the fluorescent glare of the overhead lights, the shiny floor, and the hollow bland nothingness of that space I was filled with panic. For the surgery, and for the dissection of me and the idea of my child. The cleaving of what I'd come to know as my whole self over these nine weeks.

I'd been a compliant, good-natured patient until then, but now I began weeping and clung obstinately onto the arm of the young nurse who'd wheeled me there on the gurney. She seemed surprised, her eyes wide. Her shoulders lifted into an apologetic shrug as she backed away from me.

"I'm sorry," she said. "It's just I've got to go."

I closed my eyes and forced myself to calm down. My mind drifted back to the Mediterranean, the turquoise sea, dining al fresco, the long stretch of sand that ringed the coast. And then, I thought of the note in my wallet, written with caution but also with hope. This scenario had seemed so improbable, so unlikely, and all the while, it had been inevitable.

When I woke, a doctor I'd never seen before was at my bedside. She had printed photographs that had been taken inside of my body. Looking at these images made me feel queasy and exposed.

"It looks like a grape in a straw," she said, showing me my Fallopian tube and the orb of life growing inside. (Later, when I am pregnant again and the baby books happily announce that my nine-week-old fetus is the size of a grape, I will recall this image with precision.) She said they removed the fetus and the section of my Fallopian tube where it had been lodged. I wanted to ask the doctor where that fragment of my body and those fused cells went. Had they been tossed in the bin along with the rest of the hospital's medical waste? I didn't ask because the answer would've been difficult, but I'll wonder, for the rest of my life.

A few years later there will be a damning media report claiming that UK hospitals incinerated their medical waste, including the products of conception (remains of miscarriage, ectopic pregnancies, anything under twenty-three weeks of gestation) and this, in part, helped to power their various buildings. In March 2015, the Human Tissue Authority released a statement on the disposal of these remains following pregnancy loss or termination and stated that all women should be given information on the various options for disposal and what happened next should be her choice—cremation, remains returned for burial, or, if she didn't want to be involved, sensitive incineration. Did the doctor who showed me the image of my ectopic pregnancy offer me the remains? I don't think so. Now, I regret that I didn't ask for them. It might have helped me mark this loss. Because with no remains, I couldn't be sure what I was mourning, or even if I was allowed to grieve for what was essentially only an idea. In the ensuing months, this would add a vague layer to my sorrow.

During that time of sadness, instead of completing my coursework, I researched how others grieved this intangible loss. I discovered that in postwar Japan, temples began accepting medical waste associated with fetal products from abortions, miscarriages, and, likely, ectopic pregnancies, to inter on their grounds, and to perform funeral and memorial services in their honour. The first of these memorials was built in 1955 in the Oji area of Kita-ku, and was called the Hall of Compassionate Sleep. It was the early beginnings of the Japanese Mizuko Kuyo tradition, a memorial practice now common at religious sites where parents (but more often mothers) can pay homage to their pregnancy loss—to the spirit of their lost children.

Rows of identical chubby stone babies, apple-cheeked and smiling, their heads capped in knitted red bonnets, stand together at these memorials, each one representing a loss, a significant event on a life's timeline. Women who visit the site are often well past their childbearing years because memory casts a long shadow. Japanese media has been cruel, and academics call it an invented tradition, but those little stone dolls represent a tangible expression of women's grief, and also their choices: Come into my womb again in two years, a woman writes on a small card that is left among many other messages to the unborn.

Online marketplaces have capitalized on this loss, selling trinkets that memorialize miscarriage: his-and-her keychains, each with half a tiny foot that joins when they are placed side by side; custom necklaces with angel wings; the hoped-for child's name engraved on a pendant; a Christmas ornament with the birth date, which is also the death date, embossed alongside a melancholy quote. At first, I find these souvenirs vulgar, but in time I come to see them as similar to the Mizuko Kuyo custom. It is just one of many ways to honour this ephemeral loss.

*

When I woke next there was a plain-faced woman with grey hair and glasses at my side. She wore a dark blouse buttoned up to her neck. I never learned her official role, but her presence seemed sanctioned by the hospital, and she was there to offer religious counsel to patients. She wanted me to pray with her but I declined. She was silent for a moment, waiting, maybe, for me to change my mind. After some time, she nodded curtly, as if punctuating an unspoken sentence.

"You don't need biological children," she said. "I never had any."

There was an underlying meanness to her soft-spoken manner. I turned my head away from her. I understood this moment to be the possible end of my fertility. I didn't need to hear it from a stranger.

"You could always adopt," she said before turning to leave.

The public ward in that grim mid-sized hospital was like a Greyhound bus terminal. Strangers passed through en route to other destinations; patients came and went carrying duffel bags while others read back issues of British tabloids sprawled across the uniform grey coverlets of their beds. Aging blue-haired candy-stripers pushed trolleys filled with tea and biscuits. Here, I realized, was the true English Cultural Landscape, in all its various guises—the broken, the dying, the healing, and the helpers alongside the judgmental doctor from the upper class, the pursed-lipped religious zealot, and the fierce Scottish nurse. It was Daisy, a lonely teenager who was pregnant for the second time, and her mother reading *Hello* magazine and trying to ignore that it was happening, again. It was the distraught woman, mid-miscarriage, who didn't know where she belonged.

I was discharged the next day, although I was bleeding profusely and it was difficult to walk. My insurance company called me five times during my hospital stay.

Once, in the hour after I woke from surgery. I don't know if this is why I was sent home so quickly. I hemorrhaged at the dorm while most of the students were sightseeing. My roommate stayed with me. We watched Pretty in Pink while pieces of my insides came out in chunks. At one point I bolted to the bathroom when the pain bent me in half, and when I looked into the toilet bowl I saw a semi-circle the size of a cupped palm. It was grey and pocked and looked like the surface of the moon. At first I wondered if it was somehow part of the fetus, but of course it was my placenta, rendered useless, and now free.

The efforts of life, I thought. All that work for nothing. But this isn't entirely true because years later I'll read about how researchers found fetal cells in the bodies of women long after they'd been pregnant. Some had been pregnant for only a matter of weeks, but in that time, fetal cells had intertwined with the mother's and they had stayed within her for the rest of her life. They morphed into other cells. They migrated through her body and they became cardiac tissue, beating with her heart, and they were found in her brain, which, some theorize, might shape the mother's behaviour. Some cells made pilgrimage routes to injury sites where they busied themselves repairing damage. Some fought disease. The researchers called these cells microchimerisms, named for the mythical chimera that was sometimes depicted as part human and part beast, or a variety of beasts within one body, or a conflagration of all of these things, but that never existed as a sole entity. She was an omen—storms, shipwrecks, and natural disasters followed in her wake. In many tales she breathed fire and had the head of a lion and the tale of a snake. She was mighty, but, ultimately, doomed. Her undoing was a goody-two-shoes hero and his trusted flying horse. She died of an arrow wound. The researchers named the fetal cells for her because, like the chimera, they could morph from one kind of cell to another. Similarly, the host, the mother, was both herself and her pregnancies, even when she was an old woman and the pregnancies were in her distant past, lost before viable or now children long grown. Learning about these cells, five years later, was some comfort. Most of the cells from my ectopic pregnancy had been flushed or disposed of—the grape in the straw—or maybe incinerated, but some, I'm now certain, remain with me, in my lungs, or my heart, or even my mind. We all leave our marks—in our remaindered cells, in the children we bear and the ones we don't, in rows of little stone dolls, and, for me, in the scratches on a page that form a story.

*

Andrew met me in London a week after my surgery. We walked slowly through London and one afternoon I lay down and napped on the grass in front of the parliament buildings. We drank coffee in outdoor cafés. The next week we spent time walking the white sand beaches along Ireland's West Coast. I bought an Aran sweater in Dingle. We slept under a thatched roof. I didn't know it then, but we would have other children, together. This one, though, felt as if it was all mine. Both the life and the loss.

In a week, I was back on a plane, heading home. In the departure lounge before our final flight there was a huddle of news journalists tracking a mid-Atlantic hurricane that was on its way to St. John's. Airline employees warned that our flight path might change mid-route. It wasn't something they could prepare for, they said. Our pilot said he would fly eastward and hope to land, which we did. As the two of us were ferried home in a taxi, I noticed that windows were shuttered and the streets were empty, but that the sidewalks were dry. There wasn't a breeze.

I woke early the next morning, jet-lagged and with the same dull pain in my gut, expecting devastation. But when I stepped outside the air was warm and the clouds had parted to reveal a brilliant blue sky, the sun burning a hole through its centre. Hurricane Bill, as the storm was called, had bypassed the island. The destruction and danger, the homes and lives upended, were unrealized threats.

We will continue to carry our talismans, whisper our prayers, and chant our incantations, but ultimately human beliefs hold no sway over the natural world. Not over the weather, not over the sea, and certainly not over the intricate workings of our own mysterious bodies. As the pilot had said over the crackling intercom, we must go forward and see what happens. In the ensuing years, other storms would ravage the island, ones whose names we would collectively recall. Bill was not destined to be among them. For most of the world, it was as if nothing had happened at all.

Ordinary Wonder Tales

"To what extent is the structure of the fairy tale related
to the structure of the ideal success story in a culture?"
ALAN DUNDES, Introduction to The Morphology
of the Folktale by Vladimir Propp

THE EVENTS OF THAT SUMMER happened a long time
ago, in a place far away from where I live now. This is the
setting and the time frame. Some of the plot points—let's
call them functions—have faded from memory, but this
is natural. Twelve years have passed, and, in some ways,
not that much has changed. For one, I still own some of
the clothing that I did then. Like the dress I've got on
today, which is faded and threadbare but works as a passable garment around the house. I have the same dog, too,
although he's quite old now and he was little more than
a puppy then. In other ways, though, my life is different.
I live in a city on the mainland now and I'm no longer a
student. Back then, I lived in St. John's, on the shores of
the North Atlantic, but I had relocated, along with Andrew,
for the spring and summer to a small cove near Bonavista
on an eastern peninsula of the island. This was so I could

carry out fieldwork for my dissertation in folklore. During this time, I was closely reading the work of the early twentieth-century Russian structuralist Vladimir Propp, who, in his *Morphology of the Folktale*, noted that there are thirty-one separate plot points—which he calls functions—in a fairy tale. The first is that the protagonist leaves home.

The images and scenes from that summer remain vivid because I was recording everything that happened. I took notes about my new neighbours, their comings and goings, how they lived and where, and I made appointments to visit them with my recording equipment so I could ask them questions, capturing their answers in a small silver machine I'd borrowed from the university's technology lab, and by taking notes in one of the many ringed notebooks I'd brought with me. I recorded whether they'd affixed a satellite dish to their homes so they could watch television, and what kind of art they hung on their walls. In my ringed notebooks I made a drawing of each house I visited so I became familiar with the number of windows that faced the sea on a particular house, its colour, which homes had a modern porch with chairs for sitting and watching the water and which ones had no porch at all. I was also keeping track of my observations and feelings about my environment and noted how these emotions morphed the longer I lived there. I was careful about what I wore during my interviews because this sometimes affected how the discussions with my neighbours went. If I wore something that accentuated my pregnancy, for example, this might distract the person I was speaking with and influence their answers or derail their train of thought. For this reason, I tried to avoid wearing billowy empire-waist blouses or maternity dresses when I visited a neighbour with my recording equipment. I didn't want my pregnancy to become part of the story. I was very serious then, I guess. I didn't yet understand how the baby becomes your story and envelops whoever you thought you were before they arrived. I didn't know this was inescapable. I was sharp then, but only as a scholar. In other ways, my education was just beginning.

In the months before I left for the cove, I would visit with my mentor, whose office was larger than those of other faculty members because he had so many books. He'd fashioned hallways out of his tall bookcases, and this gave the room a warren-like feel. As a young man, my mentor had done fieldwork in a small outport on the island's southern shore. He'd made maps of the paths that neighbours took between each other's homes when visiting; he'd recorded the direction their front doors faced, in which parts of their houses they tended to gather—which was, nearly always, the kitchen. It was a story of belonging. I aimed to tell a modern version of this story, one that hadn't existed when my mentor had lived on the southern shore. People from away were buying old fishing family homes for cheap and renovating them to look old-fashioned, stripping them of any modern improvements like wall-to-wall carpeting or a satellite dish. They came in summer and lived in an imagined past they and their ancestors had never experienced. If my mentor's story was about belonging, I seemed set to uncover its opposite. There is no satisfying antonym to belonging, but in this case, it was the act of standing outside a history of suffering, of you and your ancestors not having suffered enough to belong to this landscape. Suffering binds your body to the earth and water, and, also, to one another. I wanted to tell parallel stories—that of the seasonal people and the locals. To do this, like my mentor, I needed to move to a small community. I would settle, as he had settled thirty years earlier on a different shore.

My mentor told me something important before I left for the cove that summer. He said, "This is not going to happen again in your life. You won't have a chance to examine a story that interests you to the depths that you will investigate and live with this story." These were words from his mentor. He was passing them on to me. Both my mentor and his mentor were men. I am a woman, and I was pregnant. These words applied to me in a different way. I think my mentor and his mentor were referring to the intrusions of their academic careers, how teaching, meetings, and the general bureaucracy of a university can be the enemy of research, how little time there is left to slowly live with a story. In a way my mentor was correct. In the future, motherhood would prevent me from doing fieldwork to the extent that I had that summer. But in another way, he was mistaken. The story I lived became the story I examined and wrote about. Have I thought of my mentor's words every day since he shared this wisdom? Maybe that would be an exaggeration, but not a large one.

∗

Andrew and I rented an old saltbox that had belonged to the local postmistress, Violet Brown, before she'd grown old and moved into the care home in Bonavista. The house had changed hands twice since then and the present owners were an American couple who operated a bed and breakfast in a cove on the northern coast of the peninsula, but who overwintered in the home we rented. Despite their steady presence in the cove, nobody seemed to know who my landlords were. If I mentioned the Americans to my neighbours, their faces went slack and their eyes blank, as if they'd been hypnotized, or as if they couldn't understand what I was saying, or maybe as I wrote once in one of my notebooks my neighbours were *performing a peaceful resistance to the commercialization of their landscape.* After referring to our American landlords and receiving my neighbours' blank hypnotized stares in return, I would go on to describe the white clapboard saltbox with the green trim at the top of Brown's Lane, a street name that appeared on no maps and was known only to the people who lived on Brown's Lane. If a neighbour still needed prompting, I'd say, "It used to be the post office." Then, they would brighten and say, "Oh, you mean Violet Brown's house. Sure, Violet was the postmistress for nearly forty years." I would say, "Yes, that's the one," and eventually I told people we were renting Violet Brown's house and stopped using my landlords' names when describing where I lived. Now, all these years later, I can't bring their names to mind, no matter how hard I try. The Americans have disappeared from my memory, too.

Andrew's work was different than mine. He studied tree rings in an exacting and measured manner and was bewildered by my folkloric research process, which was mainly to walk our dog around the small roads that connected the five coves and meet people, only asking them for an interview after having spoken with them on several different occasions. Folklorists call this sort of thing *establishing rapport*. I'd moved around a lot as a child—sometimes to small rural places like this one—so aimless wandering and meeting people in a foreign landscape came naturally to me, although I conceded that the approach could seem opaque to those in what is referred to as the hard sciences. Meeting people and gaining their trust is hard, though, I'd pointed out. Harder, one might argue, than counting tree rings.

That summer I took a lot of naps on the grubby little couch the American landlords had left in the kitchen of Violet Brown's former home, and Andrew would jokingly ask if this was *part of my process*. It wasn't, but it was necessary because early pregnancy causes debilitating fatigue. Once, while driving home from an interview in a different cove, I had to pull my car over in the empty parking lot of what I'd believed was an abandoned building so that I could take a nap. I woke to music and the smell of grilled meat. There were several rows of cars on either side of me. It turned out I was at the local legion and while I'd been asleep many people had arrived for a party. The paint was peeling on the legion building and there was more than one missing board. It had looked forgotten and unused to me, but it was a central and lively part of the community. This was just the kind of lesson I needed to learn as an outsider, so I guess you could say that although naps weren't a planned part of the research, sometimes they helped in surprising ways.

The seasonal home owners who came to these small coves from the mainland held a different, more magical or nostalgic notion of this place than the people who lived there year-round. It was an old landscape and the migration paths were well worn. Even the earliest settlers in the tiny cove where I lived that summer had come from somewhere else a few hundred years before. They'd left Bonavista, floating their dories and houses and fishing stages along the small bays until they found this place and called it their own. Among them were the Browns. My closest neighbour, Wilson Brown, told me this, and I was inclined to believe him. He was a retired school-teacher, and eighty-two at the time. He was as keen to talk as I was to listen. We *established rapport* on the day after I arrived. He was dismantling an abandoned house across from our rental home, and, seeing me walk by with the dog he said, "This road is called Brown's Lane but there's no street sign." And then he asked, "Are you the researcher from the university?" He'd heard I was coming. From who? Oh, I don't know. The wind, or the whales, or, more likely, from Theresa who ran the Red and White store on the road to town and knew everything about everyone. She was great for finding me summer people to interview. I'd stop into the store to buy some ketchup or a litre of milk and Theresa would send me home with a new name and phone number. She kept an address book beside the cash register, the edges of its hardback cover worn soft with use. Every person who ever passed through the five coves was recorded in Theresa's book. Once, I visited the store wearing one of those maternity blouses I'd intentionally avoided during interviews and Theresa had raised her eyebrows and said, "Well, you look *some* pregnant in that shirt." Then, she'd handed me a handwritten note on a torn piece of paper with the name and number of a summer resident who'd recently bought a house in one of the coves.

I should mention that I'd completed my comprehensive exams in early spring before I'd left for the cove. I'd built a mind-ship of what defined European folklore over the last century: tales of the early Irish collectors who bicycled from town to town, wax cylinder recorders strapped to their backs; how knick-knacks on a mantle—the mantlescape—illustrate who you are, or who you want people to think you are; the way a fairy tales morphs when it travels to suit the landscape and people but the story stays the same; how female ballad singers choose their repertoire to convey coded warnings to the women and girls in their audience—messages of how to stay safe; how fairies don't have wings, but instead, look just like you and me; how you can avoid being taken away with a fairy by carrying a crust of bread in your pocket. This vessel of folk concepts, names, and theories floated on a sea of stories. Everyone's sea is made of stories, although some call them memories and, ultimately, they are the same thing. I didn't go on to teach so I don't revisit everything I learned on a ritual basis. Because of this, my mind-ship has drifted quite far, and information comes slower now, as if through fog. If I think of concepts from my studies I often need to seek out an article or book or scan an online database for some ancient conference proceedings. Even then, what I am hoping to find might remain obscure.

There are other mind-ships in my sea. There is a mind-ship for each of the two books I've written, and a third for the one I wrote in my mid-twenties that was never published and was not very good. On these ships you'll find the sunroom in the funeral home my great grandmother operated in Niagara Falls, an orphanage in Eastern Ukraine where all the children wished for roller skates, and an infant that was born so beautiful the entire hospital came to see her. There is a baby years mind-ship that carries swaddling techniques, and tips on when to introduce solid foods; directions on how to install a car seat, and how to fold a stroller so that it fits into the trunk of a sedan. Also, on this ship you will find the terrible mixture of shame and gratitude for epidural needles administered during labour. The reasons for both of these emotions have grown vague to me now. Why did we care about those needles? Why did accepting pain relief suggest we'd failed as a woman or as a human being? I could find these answers in the baby years mind-ship, but it has set sail now and I do not care to call it back in.

I'd studied nearly a year for my comprehensive exams and had achieved a level of knowledge and an accompanying confidence I haven't managed to recapture since. A day or two after my exams ended, I went to the grocery store and packed my own shopping bag faster and more efficiently than I'd ever done before. The cashier had watched me with curiosity. She'd said, "You are very good at that." It seemed my excessive studying had spilled over to other parts of my life. Or, to say it another way, my life and my studies had become intertwined. In any case, I was sensitive to patterns after all that reading, and this is why I recognized the repetitions in the summer people's stories.

*

By mid-June, I'd recorded the arrival narratives of a nun, an artist, and several different couples and each story began the same way—the protagonist, or, the hero, as they would be named in Propp's *tale roles*, left home and took a long journey. As with fairy tales, this was always the first function.

Next, through a twist of fate the hero discovered a beautiful house by the sea. Naturally, they wanted to possess this treasure. Owning the house was the narrative goal, and this success would mark the end of their story. At the outset, this seemed like a simple task because the rural homes that dotted the island's coves were inexpensive. There was a joke back then that you could buy a house with the advance on your credit card, which, apparently, some tourist did once and then never returned. In my notebook I wrote: *This rumour presents the story of a wealthy outsider commodifying a culture they feel no connection with.*

Many of the houses the summer people purchased had been uninhabited for several decades. This was because the fish had disappeared from the ocean. This sounds like a fable or a magic story but it is really just a tragedy. *The fish were casualties of industrialization*, I wrote at the time. *Also, it was not the fault of inshore fishermen based out of the island's small coves, e.g., Wilson Brown's ancestors.*

When the fisherpeople had nothing left, many of them walked away from their homes and left all their belongings inside. I think this is because they were desperate, but, also, because they hoped to return. There was a yellow house in the cove like this. It was on a severe tilt, listing east, and through the front window you could see the kitchen table and chairs as well as the kettle, untouched for decades, slowly rusting on the stove.

The summer home owners always acknowledged this tragic history in our interviews, but they never made a direct connection between their arrival and the previous owner's departure. I think this shrugging of responsibility was their fault line. It provided the crack for the villain to crawl through. In each of the stories I'd heard, the villain appeared at the point of sale or just before and introduced an indictment, preventing the hero from purchasing their summer home. The villain might be the curmudgeonly old man next door with whom the prospective buyers must negotiate a right-of-way, they might be a previous owner who takes up residence in the backyard shed, claiming he didn't agree to sell this portion of the land, or the villain might be the realtor showing the house, inflating the house price after growing suddenly suspicious of the outsider and their intentions.

In traditional fairy tales, the type that Propp analyzed for his *Morphology*, we don't tend to learn the villain's backstory. They appear fully formed and they have only one role to play. In the coves, though, I wondered, couldn't the villain be protecting what they loved? Curiously, once the house was successfully purchased, the villain almost always morphed into the role of helper. Every summer home owner had a helper. In fairy tales, the helpers facilitate the hero's journey and this is also what they did for the summer home owners. They kept the summer people's cars overwinter and picked them up at the airport when they arrived. They watched the houses during the winter months, checked appliances and set mouse traps, left their signatures and the date on forms to be used for insurance purposes. Mostly, Propp's tale roles and functions had overlaid succinctly with the arrival narratives I'd collected from the summer people, but the villain-helper dichotomy troubled me. I'd understood these roles to be opposites. I was beginning to wonder if they were, in fact, the same thing.

I gained some insight into this on the morning in late June that I interviewed my neighbours Doris and Eugene Skiffington. They lived in a sunshine-yellow house—six windows facing the sea—where Brown's Lane curved to the left and petered out into a trail through the woods that led to the swimming rock and a large patch of wild blueberries. The Skiffingtons had a small white poodle named Angel that sniffed around my ankles as I sat at the kitchen table. Doris said she wouldn't smoke while I visited because I was pregnant. Word was out by then, so it no longer mattered much what I wore. I guess, also, it was just obvious that I was expecting.

Here is something interesting about the local people I interviewed: they never, ever complained about the summer people. They had plenty of reasons to complain. For one, a summer couple had settled at the edge of the woods and they were barring locals from accessing the right-of-way that led to the swimming rock and the berry patch. I got to talking about the right-of-way with Eugene and Doris and they were evasive and took on that vague, hypnotized look

I'd seen whenever I mentioned our American landlords, as if they weren't sure what or whom I was speaking about. Finally, Doris, searching for something nice to say, told me the couple never stopped people on Ski-Doos from accessing the right-of-way in winter. I nodded and agreed that this was amenable of them, but, inwardly, I was thinking about how the summer home owners weren't there in winter and so they had no idea that the Ski-Doos zipped across their snowy lawn. Doris would know this, too, of course, but what else could she say? Then, Eugene, who was born in the house next door, whose memory stretched back to the time that his ancestors boated down the coves along with the Browns in search of new land, said something important. He told me, "You can't be bad friends."

At first, I thought he'd come up with this term on the spot, but later in our visit he repeated it. He said, "You can't live here and be bad friends." I heard this saying a few more times that summer, and I understood it to mean that if you live in a small settlement like this, no matter if you are a summer resident or a local, you must get along with your neighbours because at some point you will need to rely on them. Listening to Eugene, I suddenly understood the villain-helper dichotomy. You could play the role of the villain to an outsider but not to a neighbour. To a neighbour in these isolated coves you could only ever be a helper.

It might seem strange that I was graphing the plot points and character roles of fairy tales onto the stories that long-term tourists told about arriving in the cove, but this felt very natural to me then. It was as if the summer people were intentionally following the functions of the fairy tales I'd studied. And it's not such a stretch that these two different styles of narratives would align. I've always felt the term fairy tale doesn't quite capture the essence of these stories. Yes, they feature magical characters, but next to none of them are fairies. I prefer the term wonder tale, which is Irish in origin, for its suggestion of awe coupled with narrative. In a way, this is most of our stories. We tell ordinary wonder tales every day.

*

A few days after my visit with Doris and Eugene Skiffington, I woke up to discover that my bedsheets were soaked in blood. Andrew had left for town the night before and was set to fly to a conference in Northern Europe that night. I lay in bed and looked out the window at the grey ocean and overcast sky and I imagined myself crawling across Wilson Brown's strawberry patch to reach his front door. I didn't do this, though. I was bleeding but nothing hurt, so I sat up, dressed, shoved a book into my purse, and drove myself to the nearest hospital, which was an hour and a half away. I knew exactly where to go. It was my second time in emergency for bleeding. The first time the obstetrician on call had sent me home with a prescription for Clarithromycin, suggesting that this antibiotic would cure what he believed was an infection. He hadn't examined me and I thought this was strange, so after filling the prescription at the Walmart pharmacy I'd stood under the fluorescent lights in the vitamin aisle and carefully read the fine print on the info sheet that accompanied my pills. In the warning section I'd read that pregnant women should not take this medication because it could interfere with fetal growth and cause bone deformities. I didn't take the pills but I didn't confront the doctor either. This was the closest medical centre to where I lived that summer. The other option would be to drive three hours on a stretch of isolated highway. In an emergency, this doctor, this hospital, was all I had.

Despite his lack of diagnostics and the dangerous pills he wanted me to take, I liked the doctor. He was charismatic. He had an open face and a gentle warmth that had spread through the examining room the first time we met. He was reassuring and confident. He'd buoyed me with his humour and seemed interested in what I was doing in the small cove, so far from the university. I'd told him about my project, how I was researching the arrival narratives of the people in the cove, about the patterns in the stories they told, and about their movement in and out of this rural landscape. He was surprised to hear that you could study something like this, but he offered—and I don't think I'm inventing this part—that he knew something about arriving, about finding yourself new in an old landscape and telling the story of how you got there. Like me, he was not from the island, and he did not have a satisfying answer to the island's perpetual question, which was not where you were from but to whom you belonged. Maybe because of this I imagined that he said something about feeling like an outsider and it has since wormed its way into my own story to become a true memory.

He was rushed in our second meeting, although he told me the bad news while smiling. This was, I think, intended to be comforting, but instead it was unnerving. The problem, the doctor told me, holding my ultrasound results in his hand, was that the fetus was not growing. It was alive, yes, and the heartbeat was very strong! And this was good! But the fetus had not grown so much as a centimetre in the four weeks since the ultrasound that had been taken during my last visit to the emergency unit. This was not territory that existed in any of my mind-ships, nor had I heard such a story before, even a magic story, of a baby that lived but never grew larger than a plum. The doctor continued to smile. I asked, "How is that possible?"

No matter how hard I try, I can't remember the doctor's answer. I can't recall the details of this encounter with the doctor the way I can summon the grey-blue of Wilson Brown's coveralls or the morning light on Doris and Eugene Skiffington's sunshine-yellow house. I think this is because I felt scared and, also, because I did not record the exchange with the doctor the way I did the other plot points of that summer. It's not that I haven't spoken of this since. I have, but it has remained an oral story. I did not write it down in my field book. It was not destined to be a chapter in my dissertation. I didn't think it belonged in my research. I believed the two were unrelated. My mind-ships have drifted far enough since that I can survey them from a distance. I can see, now, how they are connected, how all parts of life weave together.

The doctor admitted me overnight for observation, and a nurse showed me to a hospital room with four beds. I chose the bed closest to the bathroom. The bed by the window had a view, but I knew what I'd see: the strip mall that sat low and squat across the highway, the coffee shop with its long line of pickup trucks idling in the drive-through, and beyond that a rise of spruce trees that stretched to the horizon. This scene was beautiful in certain lights, but I was not interested in the light. The nurse proceeded to hook me up to an IV drip and she panted as she tried and failed to insert the needle into a vein on the back of my left hand. After a struggle, she switched to my right. I asked her what the IV was for, and she said it was in case of emergency. My eyes watered from the effort of the vein search and I felt light-headed. I had called Andrew from the foyer earlier. He'd cancelled his conference and would arrive by morning. I don't remember sunset that night or dusk or what I ate for dinner or when or how I fell asleep. I do remember feeling afraid to move, and, also, I remember feeling nothing at all.

*

I'd pulled the curtain all the way around my hospital bed, so when I woke in the night, I could hear the two women but I wasn't able to see them. They were voices in the dark, but their close proximity forged an intimacy between me and them, as if I were part of their crisis. I can visualize the scene now, and when I do I can bring to mind both of the women—the patient and her sister—as if I had been watching their drama play out rather than listening from behind the curtain. As if, instead of shadows, they were fully formed bodies of flesh and eyes and mouths and limbs. I envisioned the patient's sister with dyed blond hair and large breasts. She was wearing a jean jacket, which is a detail that has always stuck with me, even though I imagined it. She was the younger of the two. I'd say the patient was not quite middle-aged, maybe approaching forty. I saw her as having black hair, like the hair of many of the women on the island, and it was wavy and shoulder-length. She wore a green hospital gown, which tied up the back and hung just below her knees. This detail is probably accurate. This is what I was wearing, too.

It was the patient's sister who had first roused me from sleep, her voice a high-pitched keen.

"Oh my god. Oh my god. Oh my god."

There was some clatter, as if someone had fallen, tripped in a rush, or maybe they'd become unsteady and collapsed.

"Oh god."

The second woman, the patient, sounded as if she was straining to speak, her voice a low moan. She continually protested her suffering. She didn't want to be a bother, it seemed.

"Sure, I'm fine," she said. "Sure, I'm okay."

"Oh my god. Oh my god. Oh my god."

"I'm okay. No, stop now. Sure, I'm fine."

"The blood. Jesus. God. I'm getting the doctor."

A third person entered the scene. It was my doctor. I knew him because I could hear the smile in his voice.

I listened as he told the patient that the bleeding was too heavy. He would not be able to stop the river of blood that ran from her body. He spoke clearly.

"You will need a hysterectomy."

"Now?"

"Yes, as soon as we can make the preparations."

The sterile light from the hall poured in and illuminated the room with a gauzy greyness. I could hear the sister now, her voice rising.

"She didn't come here to have...this operation."

The sister did not say the word hysterectomy. It was, perhaps, too violent, too final.

"I'm sorry," the patient's sister said to the doctor, and I heard her voice crack, "but what are your credentials?"

The doctor remained genial and calm. He did not sound defensive. I was able to hear him speaking in a low, confident murmur, but I could not hear what he said in response, and when he spoke again I heard the word "children" and it hovered there in the air between our two beds but I did not know exactly how it was used, or maybe I don't want to remember. I sat up and leaned closer, listening for answers, but the conversation became even more muffled, a private discussion between the sisters. The doctor was silent for so long that I thought he'd left, but then I heard the patient speaking to him in a calm, even tone, agreeing to have the surgery. I wondered if she'd been given medication. I wondered if the ham-fisted nurse had mined her veins, too, and if her saline drip had switched, now, to something fuzzier, numbing her to pain and also to emotion. After that, I heard the sounds of the patient's hospital gurney being wheeled out of the room and the patient's sister's cries became fainter and then disappeared entirely as she followed her sister down the hallway. They did not return that night.

When I was certain I was alone again, I drew the curtain back and stepped down from my bed. The other patient's bed was gone. On the floor, there was a pool of blood the size of a manhole cover. It was a great, dark lake and I dragged my IV pole along its banks, careful not to fall in.

In the early morning hours that followed, unable to sleep, I wished I was back at Violet Brown's former home taking my tea at the kitchen table, staring out to sea, which, yes, if you must know, was *part of my process*. It was strange to think that if Violet Brown was awake at this hour, she might be yearning for the same thing. I visited Violet at the care home once that summer. She sat in her shared bedroom with her purse on her lap, fastened tight as if she herself were only a visitor and might get up and leave at any moment.

Violet told me she missed her home, and she pulled out a snapshot from her purse to show me. I wasn't sure if she'd placed it in her purse in preparation for my visit or if she carried it with her always. I had no images to share with Violet of how her house had changed since she left, and this was a relief. The lilacs that had neatly framed the back door were now overgrown and the lawn had become a tangle of weeds and tall grasses. The paint was chipping on her shed, and one corner was sinking into the earth. It was a wilder space now, nature threatening to reclaim the house as it had done to so many of the old homes in the coves.

Violet asked me what her house looked like now, and I told her what I felt she could bear. I said that it was lovely but not quite as beautiful as when she'd lived there. Then, to change the subject, I told her about how I sat at the kitchen window and looked out to sea. She nodded, and smiled, and said, "I sat there, too. I did the same."

She told me she quilted by the front window, and hooked mats, but when I asked to see them she said they were all gone to the mainland. The junkmen came around and bought them all. But that didn't matter as much as her memory of hooking them, of staring out to sea.

"My dear, I sat there for hours," she said.

After that we were quiet for a moment, both of us sitting within the nondescript walls of the care home with a vision of the cove in our heads. Every day after that visit, when I looked at the ocean, I thought about Violet Brown, sitting with her purse on her lap, and I would try to transmit the image of the ocean to her, to telepathically share the rocky cliff's edge, the green fields, the scattering of old clapboard homes. I knew this was impossible and ridiculous, but I went through all manner of magical thinking that summer and this was the least of it.

For one, I suspected that the patient and her sister were spectral warnings. At first, I'd thought the sister in the jean jacket was maybe a banshee, what with her keening, but then I concluded that they were more likely a pair of wraiths, omens in human form. I know this kind of supernatural talk can make certain people uncomfortable. Men, often. They really can't stand it. Maybe they associate spirituality with femininity and they're the kind of person who can't handle either. In any case, folklorists don't believe or not believe. It's not about that. If you say there was a fairy who lived next door to your childhood home, well, then there was a fairy who lived next door to your childhood home. That is your *lived experience*.

I called my mother from the hospital the next morning using the phone beside my bed, and she said that I must have dreamed the two women out of stress, that the whole thing never really happened, but I don't think this is quite accurate. They were real, or real-ish. They existed because I existed with them. While I spoke to my mother, I was holding the phone receiver to my ear and staring down at the shiny floor of my hospital room. It had been polished to a sheen. I could have seen my own face in it. The pool of blood was gone. Someone must have mopped it up in the night.

I knew I had to leave the hospital that morning and that I had to do so before seeing the doctor for a third time. Have you heard of the law of threes? Once you know this pattern, you will see it everywhere. There are three pigs, three wishes, three sisters, but, most importantly, there are three chances. It's a narrative device that helps the storyteller remember her lines, and it works to build tension. It's also been suggested that this grouping of three—characters, events, chances—satisfies the listener and puts them at ease. These are theories. No one can say for sure why stories follow this law, just that they have for a very long time, and people have come to expect it and to feel unhinged or unsatisfied if the plot doesn't involve a trifecta of characters or functions.

Leaving the hospital wasn't as difficult as I thought it would be. Andrew arrived and after some tussle with the nurse on duty I was discharged into the care of my regular obstetrician in St. John's. She's a whole other story! Wow! She was sharp-tongued, and perpetually, almost comically aggrieved, and so I enjoyed being in her office and watching her curse and twist her mouth and roll her eyes back into her head after comparing my two ultrasound reports. The rural doctor had been looking at the wrong report, she relayed. He'd read the one from my first visit, not my second. At the time, I was outraged, too, but I'm more puzzled over this incident now. I've never been able to figure out how the doctor might miss something so obvious. Why didn't he question this strange report when the size of the fetus and the weeks of my pregnancy didn't align? Was the doctor pretending to be a doctor, and, if he was, how did he do this? He must have some medical training. But why the lack of examination, the antibiotics, the mix-up with the ultrasound reports, not to mention my roommate's unexpected midnight hysterectomy? What was missing from this story? Every time I search my memory, return to that dark hospital room, the doctor remains behind the curtain. He is a shadow I'll never fully see. My female obstetrician asked, "Who does that?" Actually, she shouted this in an apoplectic manner. Looking at my belly, she said, "He should have known by looking at you that the baby was the regular size." That's when I remembered that he'd never examined me. I told my doctor this information and she'd given me a hard stare, her mouth a firm, thin line. This time, she said nothing at all.

The thing about this story that might surprise you is that even after all the bleeding I did not lose the baby. She survived. We both did. I can't tell you why. No one was able to give me an explanation and so I stopped asking. Actually, I'd likely have forgotten about the bleeding by now if I hadn't needed to retell this story over the years. Our baby was born with a genetic condition and because of this every doctor she sees asks me about my pregnancy. Every one! Even now, and she's eleven years old. It's as if there is some mystery to be solved, something I could have done differently. If you know anything about genetics, you know there is no magic involved, although I admit it can sometimes seem this way. It can seem mystifying or preordained or linked to fate, but it's not. It's just science. In any case, the medical people still want me to haul out this old chestnut and, dutifully, I do. Each time, I tell an abridged version of the night in the hospital. The bleeding, the approximate week of pregnancy, and how I'd been admitted overnight for observation.

I leave out the other details of the story. I don't tell them about Wilson Brown's strawberry patch, or about Violet Brown who lived in the care home and how she missed the view of the ocean, or how I'd napped on that strange little couch in the kitchen of our rental home, or about any of the arrival narratives I recorded that summer. The doctors are usually in a rush. They ask for the story, but they are not prepared to sit for the length it takes to tell it. Not like the rural doctor, who'd listened, and cocked his head, and even laughed. Every time I've told this story, the faceless hysterectomy patient hovers on the margins, but I don't mention her, or the dark red pool of her blood on our shared floor, or the sounds of her sister weeping. I don't try to explain what a banshee is, or a wraith, or how these things are important to know if you are a woman navigating the medical system. The doctors are usually men, and, as I said, men do not like this kind of talk. So, I stick to the numbers and the body and generally leave feeling disappointed for not saying more.

Recently, I've been searching the internet for some of the people I knew that summer. I don't know why. Maybe because more than ten years have passed and a decade feels like a significant interval of time. I looked for Violet Brown's name online and I found her obituary. She lived for seven more years in the care home. I hope she saw the telepathic view I sent her. I haven't searched for Wilson Brown. I couldn't bear to discover his death on the internet. I'd rather go back to the place where we knew each other, however long it takes me to do this, and learn about Wilson's life or death the way I learned everything there—from the whales, or the wind, or by stopping into the Red and White store and asking Theresa. She would pull out her old book with the soft worn edges and tell me, as frankly as she'd pointed out my pregnant belly, who was passing through, who was staying put, and who had passed on.

I searched for the doctor, too, and discovered that he works at a different rural hospital now, one far from where we met but similar in its isolation. These details could be classified as facts. The rest, culled from online reviews, are harder to parse. If I was to make a note in my ringed notebook, I'd categorize the following information as rumour or gossip, but don't be confused by this, because these genres are as important to the study of folklore as

Propp's functions or tale roles. In these online stories, several people mention going in for standard surgery and coming out with a nephrostomy bag. There are two stories that recount a mistakenly cut bladder, and one incident of a cut bowel. There is a tale of a placenta left inside after a Caesarian birth and discovered several weeks later. There is more than one surprise hysterectomy mentioned, but none of them are the woman from my room as the dates and places don't match. But, then, there are patients who found him funny and warm and one person who said he gave them a second chance at life and another who said she missed him and signed her review with her initials so that if he were to come across this site he might recognize her. A new mother left a brief but touching note of gratitude: *Thank you for bringing my baby safely into the world.*

One of the final functions in a fairy tale happens when the villain is defeated. It is necessary for the hero's success so they can return home, or find a new home and, as the saying goes, live happily ever after. I've always wondered, though, where does the villain go next? Does the villain move from one story to another wreaking havoc? Can the villain change, as they did in the summer people's arrival narratives, into a helper? How do they see themselves? Maybe the villain is the hero of their own narrative. The answer, well, that's up to me and you. It depends on who we cast and how we tell the story.

Child Unwittingly Promised

1

THERE ARE TWO STORIES I want to tell you about a child unwittingly promised. I will begin by telling the earliest story, which takes place not in your time and not in my time but in a time long ago and far away. The setting is an old grist mill in Castleton, Ontario, that my great uncle owned for a period in the 1980s and '90s. The mill is two storeys tall with a peaked roof and a wooden sign, barely visible today, that spells out the name of the former owners across the façade. They were the Purdy family, but this story didn't happen in their time either. The mill is a stage set. It is the location my mind conjures when I read this fairy tale and, also, when I think about it.

The mill sits alongside a stream at the foot of a small hill. There is an apple tree in the field behind it, but only in my mind's eye. Thirty years ago, my mother's cousin ran an antique shop out of this mill. She was choosy about which items she would sell to people. If she felt the piece didn't suit the buyer—a teacup, a side table, a cuckoo clock—she would tell them it wasn't for sale. She believed each item had a rightful owner. She was more matchmaker than salesperson. Once, when I visited the shop, my mother's cousin allowed me to buy a set of dishes which I still own today. They are a soft yellow colour with a sweet pastoral pattern—a thatched cottage nestled among rolling green hills, half an orange sun peeking through fluffy clouds above.

The landscape on these dishes is the backdrop for the first story of the child unwittingly promised. The pattern is what you might see in the distance if you were standing and facing the old mill, which is where the story opens. The first person to appear in this story is the miller, but I do not cast my great-uncle in this role. My great-uncle was sweet and kind, while the miller is a greedy, clueless man whose features aren't altogether clear to me, a hint of a face above blue coveralls. The miller, who lives with his wife and their teenage daughter, has fallen little by little into poverty, but we don't learn why. As in most fairy tales, all that happened before the traditional opening line is meaningless. The action is immediate and linear, contained within the tale. There is no past to consider, no narrative flashbacks to give context. These details are up to the listener to fill.

One afternoon, the miller decides to go to the forest to chop some wood. Perhaps he could sell some kindling, he thinks. Maybe he could sell it in bundles along the roadside, the kind you see in crates at the foot of country lanes with painted signs alerting passersby that there is firewood for sale.

In the woods the miller meets an old man he's never seen before. This old man says he'll buy what lies behind the mill and in exchange the miller will receive a lifetime of wealth. This has the ring of a get-rich-quick scam, or at the very least a pyramid scheme, but, as I mentioned, the miller is greedy and this tends to cloud his logic. The miller does a brief mental inventory of what lies behind the mill—grass, earth, what else? Oh, there's the old apple tree. Well, he can do without apples, he thinks. He agrees to sell, and the old man hands him a pen and a contract to sign. The miller signs the form and hands it back without reading the terms and conditions, maybe because he's illiterate and he can't, or maybe because he's careless. The old man folds the contract neatly and tucks it into a pocket of his windbreaker.

Back at home (which I imagine to be the thatched cottage from the yellow dishes) the miller finds his bewildered wife on the doorstep. She has come outside to escape her house because it is brimming with gold coins from every drawer, closet, and cupboard, and she does not understand how or why, but she has a bad feeling that her husband is involved and that the money is dirty. She doesn't say this outright, but you can read between the lines when she says, "Tell me, miller, how did all this wealth suddenly get into our house?" She's obviously ready for an argument because she doesn't use his proper name, which we don't know, but, surely, she does.

The miller is focused only on his good fortune, and he shrugs off his wife's accusatory tone.

"A stranger in the forest promised me great wealth if I agreed, in writing, to give him what's behind our mill," he says. I envision him smiling broadly as he tells her this.

I see the wife turning away from the miller when she responds, so that she's facing the rolling green hills, the puffy clouds, and the orange sun in the porcelain-yellow sky.

"You fool, our daughter was sweeping behind the mill," she tells her husband. "You've promised her to the devil."

2

The second story begins in a genetic counsellor's office at the Victoria General Hospital on Vancouver Island. The office has high ceilings, pale green walls, and a bank of windows that face a stand of white pines. I am sitting beside my husband on one side of a narrow wooden desk, and on the other side are a genetic counsellor and a student trainee who is shadowing her. My husband and I offer information about our medical histories as the student trainee draws our intertwined family trees, using circles to represent females and squares for males. Some of the circles and squares are marked with an X to indicate that they carry a known genetic mutation. I am an X, my husband is an X, and our daughter is an X, although her circle is shaded to indicate that she has expressed the mutation. She has albinism, which means she lacks pigment in her hair, skin, and eyes, and that she is legally blind. The first X on my family tree is a cabinetmaker from New England who moved to Niagara Falls, Ontario, at the beginning of the nineteenth century and founded a funeral business. The cabinetmaker lived not in my time and not in your time but in a time long ago and far away; however, like my uncle's former mill, the funeral home remains today and I've been there enough—for memorial services only, as my family sold the business in the 1970s—that I can visualize my ancestor's interior world without too much effort.

I'd tracked him down after my daughter was born because I knew nothing about albinism, and I thought my ancestors might offer some insight. I'd slowly drawn the branches of our tree using information gleaned by scientists who studied our blood and spit, and, less dramatically, by telephoning distant relatives who'd never heard of me, by scouring archives and old newspaper records, and by poring over the disintegrating family photo albums that my father inherited from the funeral home. I collected each X as if it marked a treasure, as with old pirate maps.

Although the mutation that my husband and I carry in our genes is recessive, we cannot draw an X in any of the circles or squares that represent his family because their records are not as vast as ours. This is partly true. It is also true that my husband's need to know the path of our mutation was not as fierce as mine. I say need, because that is how it felt to me. Looking back, I understand that this urge to uncover what I could not see was actually a want. It was a choice I made, and, as with any information, once revealed, it could not be forgotten. It would always be a part of our story.

My daughter is three now and I am pregnant again. We have moved across the country since her birth, so this is a different genetic counsellor, office, and hospital than the first time around. Despite these changes, the circles and squares, and the questions they elicit, are nearly identical.

Once the trainee has finished completing our family tree, she hands it to her superior so we can discuss what we might do next. The genetic counsellor gives us two choices. The first is that I can undergo amniocentesis, a procedure in which a needle draws amniotic fluid from my womb that can then be tested for the mutated gene. After receiving the results, we can opt to terminate or continue with the pregnancy. The second is that we can forgo the test and adopt a wait-and-see approach. The second is the safest option. Having the test offers us the information we want, but it comes with a risk, albeit small, that I might miscarry. While this weighs on me, my pursuit of knowledge overrides my fear. I am greedy for information. I can have what I want, but there is a cost.

"Don't be alarmed by this," the counsellor cautions, pointing out a line on the consent form that suggests we will change the management of our pregnancy if the test comes back positive for the mutated gene. The euphemistic wording makes it sound as if we are choosing a home birth rather than a hospital birth, or perhaps opting for a midwife over an obstetrician, but it is nothing so benign. It means that we will terminate the pregnancy if the result is positive. The counsellor tells us that this caveat is related to funding. The provincial government does not fund in vitro testing for parents seeking knowledge, like us, only those seeking action. Determining whether your baby will have a genetic condition as a means of preparing for that child is not deemed necessary or cost effective.

"Don't worry," the geneticist says. "They don't hold you to it."

She says this with a little laugh, and at first I think this is because she is uncomfortable, but then I wonder if she's not actually laughing, if maybe she's baring her teeth. She is a white woman, with straight blond hair, and I would guess that she is in her late thirties. She looks like she might be a jogger, although I can also picture her on one of those stand-up paddleboards I see people using in the bay when I walk the dog in the mornings. Outside the window the pines bend in a gentle wind. We are, technically speaking, in the woods. Her ordinariness could be the perfect disguise. Maybe she's the devil and by signing this form we are making an unwitting promise.

3

Three years later the devil comes for the miller's daughter. I picture the young maiden waiting for him on the bank of the stream that runs alongside the mill. She has immersed herself in this water, in preparation. She then draws a circle with white chalk on the ground and steps inside. From where the maiden stands, meaning from where I've positioned her in my mind, she can see the devil as he turns onto Mill Street, passing my great-grandmother's house—the green saltbox with the white trim—as he rounds the corner.

He approaches the maiden with such speed, such smug confidence, that he is momentarily bewildered when he finds himself unable to touch her. The maiden has no agency over her own life. She has been sold without the ability to protest, given away without her consent, so she has turned to magic as a defence. It was an unlikely bet—she must have known this—but it has worked. The devil's confusion quickly gives way to rage, one so fierce and hot that it evaporates all the water from the world.

"There," he says. "Now you cannot wash. I'll be back for you tomorrow."

But when he returns for the maiden the next day, she's wept her hands safe. Her tears are impenetrable. The devil finds for the second time that he cannot take hold of her. He knows what to do. He seeks out her greedy, cowardly father.

"You better cut your daughter's hands off," he tells the miller. "Or I'll come for you instead."

This part is difficult to understand, and, also, to envision. The daughter remains calm, holds her hands out to her father. They stand in the interior of the mill, but not in its incarnation as the antique shop. It is in its present form, which is to say, it is abandoned, and the windows are boarded shut. The space is dimly lit and shadowy. It has an uneven, earthen floor. I see the old millstone, lying inert, on its side. It has become a butcher's block. The maiden lays her arms across the stone, but at the last moment I turn away so I can't describe this scene. You will need to imagine it yourself.

She is betrayed and mutilated by her father, harassed by the devil, but, astonishingly, the maiden persists. She weeps into her ghost hands, her bloodied stumps, and, when the devil arrives for this third attempt, he finds that she is a fortress. He cannot touch her. He cannot take her home with him. The devil storms away, disappears into the bush off a dead-end road. He has given up on her, for now, but the maiden is not safe. Not at home with her father. The miller stands at the door to his thatched-roof cottage. The clouds have parted and the orange sun is relentless in the hard-yellow sky.

"Come home," he says, holding the door ajar. "We are rich now, and you are free."

The maiden knows only one of these statements is true. She turns away from him. She walks into the rolling hills and never comes back.

4

The summer that I am pregnant with our second child, I drive to California with my husband and our daughter to attend a conference in San Diego. The conference is for people who share my daughter's genetic condition as well as their families, and this is our second time at the gathering since our daughter was born. At the end of the trip, we have planned that my husband will drive home alone while my daughter and I will fly back to Vancouver Island without him.

On the final morning of the conference, after my husband begins his drive home, I meet an old woman in the lobby of the hotel. I am standing in line with my daughter, waiting to check out of our room, and the old woman, who is sitting in a chair by the wall, waves me toward her in a way so familiar that I wonder if we know each other. She is wearing a pastel-blue cardigan and a long denim skirt. Her white hair is swept into a bun. She nods at my daughter.

"I saw you across the room and I knew that I wanted to meet you," she says to her.

After speaking to my daughter, she lifts her eyes to meet mine. She tells me that her adult daughter has albinism, and that this was their first time at the conference. She asks if my daughter is my only child. For now, I tell her, but we are expecting our second in December.

"The baby is due on my daughter's birthday," I say. This is a superfluous detail, but I am hopeful that it will work to re-include my daughter into our conversation. It does not.

The old woman congratulates me, and then she pauses for some time, fixing her gaze on something just beyond my shoulder.

"I had another child," she says, after a long silence. "A son. He also had albinism but he died at six months of crib death."

I tell her that I am sorry. I speak in a careful, measured tone, but my voice tremors and I feel as if I might lose control. The sensation is unexpected. I fear that I may weep, or, worse, howl, and be unable to stop and it will all happen here in this crowded hotel lobby with my daughter by my side. There is no heightened risk of crib death for children who have my daughter's condition, none that I know of, but it is difficult not to equate this story with my own situation, my own baby, particularly after the woman has made a point of drawing parallels between our two lives. Still, I feel that my reaction is strange and too large for the situation. The old woman doesn't seem to notice my problems, or maybe she is unbothered. She might think it an appropriate response to her tragedy.

"Being here over the past few days, I saw all these little boys and teenagers who looked the way he might have looked, and the adults, the grown men who'd be about his age now," the old woman says, and she makes a sweeping gesture with her arm, as if to summon the boys and men. "It was difficult, but I also felt close to him here. Closer than I have in a long time. I felt his presence."

"That must feel—"

I can't find the right word to describe such a thing, but the old woman nods, and says, "yes," as if I have finished my sentence with the perfect explanation of how she'd felt. The line is growing longer at the front desk, and although my urge to weep has subsided, I feel unbalanced and tired, ready to finish this social exchange. I excuse myself and my daughter and say goodbye.

After checking out of our hotel we have an entire day to wait for our flight home. To entertain my daughter, I take her to an outdoor shopping mall. It is the only place we can walk to from the hotel. At the mall, there is a fenced-in Astroturf play area for young children. It has a slide, some garish plastic animals on springs that rock back and forth when you sit on them, and a small swing set. I sit on one of the benches that line the periphery of the play area. This is where all of the mothers sit, watching their children. The other mothers, who are presumably locals, look wealthy, and most are younger than I am. They are tanned, and wear gold bangles and necklaces and large hooped earrings. They carry small purses. What fits in those small bags, I wonder? What about the containers of Cheerios and the water bottles? What about the crayons and paper? Where do those things go?

As I watch my daughter spring back and forth on a shiny plastic pig, I think about the old woman we met that morning. I imagine the woman sitting at one of the round tables in the conference buffet room, watching for men of a certain age. What do they offer her? A glimpse of something impossible, a different option, one that was never offered, never available for her. What word could you use to capture the feeling of coming close to your lost child? Comfort, maybe. Hopeful, perhaps, despite knowing otherwise, that you might chance on a dimension where your child lived. Is there a word for a hope like this? Is it nostalgia but for something that never came to pass? No, that's not quite right either. Then, it comes to me. She must have felt consoled. Yes, this is the word I had been seeking, the word that would have filled the blank space in our conversation. The old woman felt consoled.

My daughter moves onto the swing. She wants me to push her. She is searching for the mother-shape that is me, amidst the other mother-shapes on the benches. I get up and walk across the Astroturf until I am close enough for her to see me. She kicks her small legs in greeting. I position myself behind her and pull the swing back as far as I can, and then I let her go.

5

The maiden wanders until dusk. She finds herself in a stand of pear trees that belong to the king which I envision as the four fruit trees that grow in the yard of our rented bungalow in Victoria, where we've lived for nearly three years. The maiden is hungry so she eats a pear right off the branch, despite knowing, somehow, that the fruit is counted nightly and the missing pear will be noticed. The next night, she returns again at dusk for another pear, but this time the king waits for her. He's in the living room of our bungalow, watching her through the sliding glass doors that lead to the back deck. You wouldn't know he was there because all you can see is the reflection of the branches and the purple-blue sunset. This is an ongoing tragedy at our home. No matter how many black silhouetted decals we paste on those doors, birds keep flying into the glass. The king watches the maiden and he finds her lovely, out there, gnawing the pears straight off the branches of his trees. He slides the patio door open, breaking the silence of the night. The crows that live in our compost heap scatter.

"Have I hallucinated you?" he asks her. "Are you a spirit or a human being?"

"I'm not a spirit," she says. "I'm just self-reliant."

The king finds the maiden captivating. He wants to marry her. She accepts this fate. Does the maiden find the king captivating? My hunch is that this doesn't matter. If she feels the king is too old for her, or hideous, or simply boring, she does not have the power or resources to refuse him. This is an act of fate, but one that it is prescriptive rather than romantic. If she hadn't met the king, she would have been tethered to some other man through a financial transaction orchestrated by her father, which, in a way, is what led her to the king. We never learn how the maiden feels. By the next sentence she is pregnant and the king has left for battle. He has asked his old mother to care for his wife, and to send word when the baby arrives.

The maiden gives birth to a boy and names him Sorrowful. This is a beautiful name, but I question the choice. I would worry that it might be predictive, that a child might grow into a name like that.

The old woman sends a message to her son—*You have a new baby boy!*—a missive of joy that is intercepted by the devil. He's never been able to move past his defeat, to accept that the maiden's witchy magic was stronger than his. He writes a new letter, forging the old woman's hand.

Your wife gave birth to a changeling.

The king is worried by what he reads, but he does not respond the way the devil hopes.

Take care of them, he writes to his mother. But the devil rips up the note, writes a fresh message.

Kill them both. Keep her tongue and eyes as proof.

The old woman is disturbed by her son's response. I imagine her in my grandmother's bedroom, standing at the tall south-facing window as she makes her decision to intervene. She will kill a doe herself and cut out its eyes and tongue. She will immerse the eyes and tongue in a jar filled with pickling fluid and store it in the root cellar.

The old woman wakes her daughter-in-law with blood-wet hands.

"Go out into the woods with your child and never come back," she tells her. This might be the hardest thing she's ever done, this disobedience, the murder of the doe, setting the maiden and her child free. She watches them walk away in the dark. I stand with her.

Sorrowful is tucked into a soft green carrier, the one with the leaf pattern on the reverse that I bought for the new baby. I see that he is wearing the striped cap that my sister knit for my daughter when she was born, as well as the matching booties. Oh wait, I think, remembering that those booties always fell off. I want to call after the maiden to tell her this, but I can't interrupt the story. Besides, I am too far away for her to hear me.

6

I am lying in the dark surrounded by a forest of green bodies. Above where I lie, the half-moon of a surgical lamp is suspended from the ceiling, illuminating my body on the table. The attending doctor is a green man with a tiny miner's lamp strapped to his head, a blinding star whose light will act as his guide. There is an ultrasound machine placed on my belly and the baby's heartbeat drums through this small, crowded space. The other greenbodies are students and nurses and the ultrasound technician.

"It's time," the green-man doctor says and I turn my head to the side because I don't want to see the doctor's needle. In the dimness my gaze is met by a set of eyes, trained on mine.

"I'm hot," I whisper to the eyes.

"I'm here," the eyes whisper back.

The eyes place their cool palm on my forehead. At the same time, I feel the needle pierce the skin of my belly. The pain makes me gasp but more unsettling is the pressure, a tugging and a shoving, meeting with resistance. There is a problem. I understand this from the green-man doctor's murmured consultation to the students and nurses, and from his tone. And, then, also, there is the fact that the needle has been pulled out again. This seems too quick to have drawn fluid.

A scattering of pinpricks spreads across my scalp. The eyes are calm and remain fixed on my face, their palm cool and steady on my forehead.

"It didn't work," the eyes tell me, gently. "The uterus wouldn't let them in, so they will need to try again."

Half an hour earlier, I'd stood under the fluorescent lights of the hospital hallway with the genetic counsellor—who I once believed was the devil in disguise, but who may simply be yet another bureaucrat. I'd held a letter from the hospital up for her to read. I'd opened the letter the night before, late, after my daughter and I arrived home to Victoria from the conference in San Diego. In it were instructions on how to prepare for the amniocentesis test, and to let me know when I should expect the results.

"I don't understand the timing." My head was buzzing. I felt drowsy and tired from travelling. "It says the results will take six weeks."

"That's right," the counsellor said, in a careful, measured tone.

"But, I'll be almost six months pregnant by then, so what if I'd wanted to *change the management?*" I asked, using the euphemism for abortion I'd learned in her office.

"We'd need to investigate other options."

I stayed silent, then, for an uncomfortably long time. Not because I didn't have anything to say, but because a heavy sorrow weighed on my words. I looked down at the floor rather than at the counsellor. It was as shiny as a lake, and the tubed ceiling lights reflected down its middle like a median line on a highway. I wanted to ask a number of questions, such as: Why had I been forced to make this promise? Was it a test? A trick? A threat? Why, if it had been a ruse, had I been required to sign away my child? Was that what she'd meant, with that odd laugh, when she'd said, "They don't hold you to it"? Had the form, and my signature, been meaningless from the beginning? If so, why make women agree to these violent terms? Why make them sign away their babies, even in theory?

I noticed a crease of consternation forming between the counsellor's brows. Our genetics are tangled and feral, and the more I understood about my human self the wilder I became. Knowledge had illuminated the forest that lives within me. It had revealed the intimate network of roots and branches, vines and weeds, all interwoven and impossible to tame. Alive, yes, but also ancient and connected to ghosts. I sensed that the counsellor knew that I was upset, but she remained silent, too. I wasn't able to ask her any of my questions, anyway. The nurse at the registration desk called my name. The procedure room was ready.

The needle enters my womb on the second attempt. It is a sharp starburst of intrusion. My heart beats fast, out of step with the baby's heart. I feel bile in my throat.

Throwing up would be a problem because I'd been told to hold absolutely still. I work together and against my body at the same time.

"Breathe," the eyes say, in a clear, even tone. "Breathe," they repeat, until the pressure eases, and the needle is removed from my body.

After the procedure, I am taken to a recovery room where I lie on my left side. The eyes come with me.

"You seem as if you might faint," the eyes say, looking concerned. As I lie there, the eyes hand me three vials of straw-coloured liquid, still warm from being inside my womb.

"I want you to check that all your information on the labels is correct," the eyes say. "This part is really important. Read each one back to me."

I wonder if in the future, amniocentesis will be cited in medical history books as a once popular but rather barbaric way of testing for genetic conditions. One that will surprise young people; they will be shocked at what we once signed away in exchange for knowledge. Some new technology will arrive in its place, of course, with its own inherent violence. Women will keep using their magic to survive, to persist. I turn the vials over in my palm so that each label faces up. I read my name out loud three times and it sounds like an incantation.

7

The maiden and Sorrowful come to a clearing in the forest, which I see as a campsite on the banks of the Skeena River, near Hazelton in northern British Columbia. It's where we camped the summer that I was pregnant and my daughter was three, about a month after we returned from the conference. The maiden finds a cottage in the clearing, and I picture it as the A-frame log cabin where my grand-mother's friend Violet lived in her old age, and so the window boxes are dripping with the yellow and orange nasturtiums that she planted every year and I can faintly hear the propeller of Violet's wind-powered electricity.

The cabin door is open and a magic woman waits there for the maiden. She is a healer-woman, an artist-woman. She has painted an enchanted sign that only the maiden can read. It is an encrypted welcome. Implicitly, the maiden knows that she and Sorrowful will be safe here.

The cottage has everything the mother and child need, and the magic woman encourages them to move in with her, and so they do, and they are both happy here. At night you can hear the gravelly whoosh of rock slides on a faraway mountain, as we could when we camped in this spot, and the sound of the river racing over the stones, and you can also see the stars. Every single one! They eat salmon and wild berries and sometimes the magic woman visits the shops in Hazelton and returns with lemon tarts, and squares of dark chocolate, loaves of sesame-crusted egg bread and fresh ground coffee.

I'm not saying the maiden should forget about the king and stay here forever, and, in the version of this story that I know best, this notion is never suggested. But, if you ask me, I think that when the maiden is an old woman she will remember this seven-year period, here on the banks of the Skeena, living with the magic woman and Sorrowful, as the best of her life.

8

You should know that I have modified the maiden's story where I felt I could get away with it, but, also, that this doesn't make it any less genuine. Everyone tells it differently. There are so many versions, and not just the hundreds found in Germany. There are thirty-three recorded variants in Japan.

One person who told this tale was named Marie. She was a storyteller but she's become marginalia. She lives today as a name and date scrawled in the white space beside the maiden's story in the original manuscript of Jacob and Wilhelm Grimm's *Children's Household and Fairy Tales*. It was March 10, 1811, when Marie told Jacob the maiden's story. Marie was twenty-three. Ringleted and bright-eyed, she'd woken transformed and vivacious after a prolonged childhood illness. The stories gleaned from books as well as her parents and visitors, and maybe from nursemaids (although this is said to be folklore), were the silver lining of her many years spent in bed. She set these tales to memory. She must have retold them to herself as a way of learning their twists, their characters and plots, and probably as a form of entertainment. Maybe she regaled her little sisters and brother with these stories, drawing them to her bedside, keeping their company for just a little longer.

As with so many women before and after her, storytelling was Marie's survival skill. She tweaked and she invented as she drew on the stories from her combined German and Huguenot ancestry. Some say that she is largely responsible for the French influence that runs like a river through so many of the Grimm fairy tales. She was greatly influenced by the stories in Charles Perrault's *Histoires ou contes du temps passé*, also known as Mother Goose Tales, which was printed in Paris in 1697. Like the Grimms, Perrault also collected oral folk tales from anonymous women and then published them under his own name.

These storytellers are a succession of women, a recital of women, a chorus of women. I can hear their voices singing through the crowded text. I can see their sleight of hand. I see it in the maiden's assured self-confidence, her pluck, that she eats when she's hungry, how she was traumatically maimed and yet she persists; and I can see it in the old woman's decision against violence, in the magic woman helper, in the agency of all the women in this story, despite the caged world within which they exist.

The images that I see, however, are my own. They are of my present and my past, a collage of my personal landscapes. What flickers to life in my mind's eye as I read or listen to a story comes unbidden. I could no more conjure them on purpose than I could stop them from appearing. They run like tickertape even as I record my own version of the maiden's story. Telling, reading, hearing, imagining, writing—together these acts are a collaboration carried out across geographies and through centuries, between the dead and the living, between intimates and strangers, between people who live and breathe and those who live only on the page, and, also, between you and me.

9

I am seven months pregnant when I see the eyes again. I have returned to the hospital for bloodwork. I am sitting in an examination room, the same place where I'd held the three warm vials of my amniotic fluid. I'm staring at my phone when the eyes walk in. I look up and remember them immediately. I remember their cool palm on my forehead. The eyes remember me, too, and, for a nearly imperceptible moment, they seem startled by my presence. They act as if they have seen a ghost.

"It's so nice to see you again," the eyes say, then they pause, and look at me, really look at me as if trying to see through me to the other side, before adding, "at this stage in your pregnancy."

I feel uncomfortable, but in the moment I can't place what is making me uneasy. I'm not able to interpret the pause, the prolonged stare, or the statement that followed.

The eyes break the silence.

"You look better than you did the last time I saw you."

We both laugh, awkwardly.

Driving home, I reflect on the strange phrasing the eyes had used. *At this stage in your pregnancy.* What stage, exactly, I wonder? Nearly to term. Past the point where you could consider changing the management. Outside, the soft green landscape of Vancouver Island rolls by in a mist. I can just make out the points of the sword ferns that march along the roadside, the knotted twists of the Rocky Mountain juniper shrubs, and, beyond this, the

Gary Oaks, their trunks, branches, and bark engulfed by the English ivy that is slowly killing them. I've always thought that if humans instantly vanished from this island it would take nature about half an hour to reclaim what we'd left behind.

I return to thinking about the examination room, to the eyes, and a troubling thought crosses my mind. The eyes know that I have unwittingly promised away my child (my son, I know his gender now) but that I have kept him, regardless. How could the eyes know my test results? How could they know that the baby is positive, a carrier, an X, just like his mother and father, but will not express the gene like his sister? The eyes do not know these details, of course. But they know one thing about me, and it is the same piece of information they know about every woman who has undergone that test, every woman whose gaze they have held in theirs—all of us signed that form. Is this what the eyes were looking for, when they stared at me in the examination room, some kind of admission? Or could it have been empathy? I don't know. Maybe I imagined their look of surprise. Maybe I was just hungry.

10

The king returns after seven years at war to find that his mother has killed his wife and child. I picture the king and the old woman sitting at my grandmother's octagonal kitchen table, the mason jar between them—the lolling tongue and watchful eyes suspended in liquid that has yellowed over time. The king lowers his head and weeps.

The old woman crosses her arms and raises her eyebrows. She has now come to occupy my grandmother's body, so she is wearing a V-neck powder-blue sweater from Talbots and a pair of tan slacks. She embodies my grandmother's voice, too, a stern tone that no one ever questioned or fought against.

"Go into the woods," the old woman says to her son, in an echo of her statement to the maiden. "They are alive there."

After a days-long search the king finds the maiden and Sorrowful at the cottage on the banks of the Skeena River. The king doesn't recognize the maiden because he is distracted by his hunger—he took a dramatic vow that he wouldn't eat until he was reunited with his family, something he no doubt regretted after a few days in the woods. The magic woman intervenes and vouches for the maiden, and the family is happily reunited. I feel a tug of regret about the cleaving of the union between the maiden and the magic woman, but this is not a plot point that I can tweak, so I will have to let it happen. There is, however, a moment where Sorrowful obstinately refuses to believe the king is his father. He is keen on his mother. He doesn't want any intrusions or distractions muddling their relationship, certainly not of the romantic, or maybe just the male, kind. He's seven now. He wonders, reasonably, "If you're my father, where have you been all this time?"

I had camped with my family on the banks of the Skeena that summer because we were on our way to a wedding in

Smithers, about an hour's drive south. This is why, after the king is reunited with the maiden, and they decide to marry a second time in celebration, I conjure the log cabin lodge where our friends were married. It has one great room, a peaked roof, and it sits at the end of a dirt road, opposite a small lake. The blue hump of the Hudson Bay mountain lies on the horizon.

Now, I see us at the maiden and king's wedding dinner. We are near the back of the crowded room, sitting with a few other families at a large round table covered in a white tablecloth—me, my daughter, my husband, and my son, still tucked inside, of whom we understood so little then. I don't know this yet, but when my son is eleven months old we will leave Vancouver Island and move across the country again, for what I hope is the last time. I will immediately register my son with the new health-care system and snip his previous identification cards into tiny pieces. Sometimes, though, I won't be able to stop myself, and I will think of the form that sits in a filing cabinet in what I see as a dark, vine-covered storage space, cobwebbed, and without light, deep in the recesses of the hospital that is surrounded by a white pine forest. I will remember my signature on a dotted line, and I will imagine, hope for, a fire.

The wedding hall is stuffed with alpine flowers— roseroot, pink mountain heather, glacier lily, and arctic lupine. The wooden floor is polished to a gleam, and fairy lights are strung overhead. I take a sweep of the great room, surveying the wedding guests, and I see the devil at a corner table. He's in disguise, in the body of a drunk uncle this time, that wedding archetype—the drunkle—there for the open bar, the party. It seems the devil has acquiesced, finally, in the heady happiness of the second marriage celebration. He has decided to leave the maiden alone. He orders another drink and slips into the crowd. The genetic counsellor is at a table across from ours and she lifts her glass and nods at me before turning back to the green-man doctor, whom she's brought as her date. The magic woman wanders by, arm in arm with the eyes.

I notice that the bride's parents aren't here, the miller and his wife. Of course, the maiden wouldn't want them to be a part of her celebration. But I do see the old woman from the conference, sitting at one of the round tables. She's swaying gently to the music. There's a faraway look in her eye, although she appears content. I notice that the seat beside her is empty. I know that this spot is reserved for her son, but I cannot conjure him. Not the infant that she knew and lost, and not the man he might have grown into. I can't say for certain, but I think this is because he lives only in her mind's eye. I can't see the old woman's son here because I can't see him anywhere. He is not mine to imagine.

The music gets louder, and the twice-married couple takes to the dance floor. Sorrowful, whose new life is just beginning, joins them, and then one after another, we get to our feet, and begin to dance, all the people from the two stories of the child unwittingly promised, including me, my husband, and our daughter. I can see this just as perfectly as if we are there again, or there for the first time, together, in the final scene of this fairy tale.

Giving up the Ghost

AFTER HE DIED, I BEGAN to see my brother with surprising frequency. These appearances were not ghostlike apparitions, nor were they dreams. Instead, I saw him in the bodies of strangers. He was waiting for the traffic light to turn so he could cross at a busy intersection. A man tipped his hat skyward to read a street sign and my brother's face hovered beneath the brim. He was the token collector at the subway entrance, the lone soup-eater in the basement food court of a downtown shopping mall.

I couldn't anticipate these visitations. They happened at random, and unexpectedly. The people I'd imprinted with my brother's image were only shades of him—dark hair, a downward slope to their shoulders, a bushy moustache, thick-rimmed glasses. This was fitting because, even in life, I didn't know him well. My brother was eleven years old when I was born, and we had different mothers. As a child he'd visited on weekends with my other brother. We'd overlapped in adulthood only briefly, so my memories of him are fleeting and jumbled. It was only after my brother died that I discovered his first name had been Joseph, a name chosen by his mother but secreted away after birth in favour of his middle name. I learned this from my father when I was tasked with writing my brother's obituary. I remember feeling both awed and ashamed that I could have spent twenty-four years in my brother's orbit but not known his given name. This was just one of the ways I didn't understand who he was. This unknowing compounded the loss, which was tragic and grim, and I think this is why I bumped into him so often after he died. When he was alive, I never ran into my brother in the city where we both lived.

I was young then, my footing in the world unsure and sometimes timid. When my brother died, I was a few weeks into my second year of a graduate program in journalism. I believed I would never return to school and that I would never write again. I felt suspended among wilted funeral flowers and well-intentioned casseroles with a grief that would last indefinitely. But after two weeks I left my parents' country home and returned to the city, resumed my studies, and re-entered my life. My upstairs neighbour serenaded me when I arrived at my apartment, assuming all the cards and flowers that had collected at my front door were birthday greetings. I thanked him, gathered the well-wishes, and stepped back into my old life, which was physically and structurally the same, but emotionally rearranged.

I don't remember the first time I saw my brother in a passing stranger, but I do know that it went on for years. I didn't investigate why these sightings happened, or if they happened to anyone else. It would take another two decades for me to do this. I am middle-aged now and a mother. I'm a more confident version of my earlier self. I'm a journalist rather than a trainee, and a folklore scholar. I interview people about their supernatural experiences, respecting their beliefs, no matter how far they stray into otherworldly terrain. I am no longer afraid to question myself.

✳

Seeing the dead is a common part of the grieving process, one that has been explored in psychiatry, religious studies, sociology, gerontology, and anthropology. These experiences happen across cultures and in different landscapes and geographies. People in cities are just as likely to see their deceased loved ones as those living in the countryside, and these sightings happen regardless of education level or gender. More women report having visions of the departed, but this might be because women tend to live longer and many of the studies I've read focused on the experiences of widows. The research papers were published in the twentieth and twenty-first centuries, but lovers reunited in bereavement is a mythological trope throughout time—from the classic Grecian tale of Orpheus and his doomed attempt to retrieve his wife, Eurydice, from the underworld, to the dead bridegroom who made off with the bride in Old Norse mythology, to Patrick Swayze and Demi Moore in the nineties movie Ghost. For every malady of the human psyche there is a folk tale, and grief provides no exception.

In the parlance of psychiatry these sightings are referred to as grief- or bereavement-hallucinations, or post-bereavement hallucinatory experiences (PBHE). But it's a phenomenon most kindly described by the neologism idionecrophany, which pairs the Greek words for private and death with the verb "to appear," a neutral term that avoids defining whether the apparitions are real or not. Because what is real—what we *believe*—can be highly subjective. I might believe in fairies and you might believe in God and another person might think both ideas are ridiculous, but in matters of faith, who is to say which of us is right or wrong? The difficulty inherent in metaphysical experiences is that believing in God is acceptable in North American society but seeing your dead brother at the dog park is considered taboo and strange, possibly pathological.

This is likely the reason that post-death visions tend to be underreported. Three separate group studies of mourners from Sweden, the United Kingdom, and the United States found that nearly all of their respondents had seen their dead loved ones in some way, but that less than half had mentioned these experiences to a living person. In interviews the bereaved parties said they feared being ridiculed, or upsetting relatives, or inviting bad luck and further tragedy. Like the study participants, I also didn't tell anyone about encountering my deceased sibling in the weeks, months, and years after his death, and for some of the same reasons: I was leery about sharing my post-death visions with friends who might not believe me, and I didn't want to further burden my grieving family. Above all, however, I worried that telling would prompt some kind of medical intervention. Seeing my brother wasn't unsettling, but the act of hallucinating and the psychiatric turmoil it implied scared me.

In the introduction to his 2012 book *Hallucinations*, Oliver Sacks wrote that "in modern Western culture, hallucinations are more often considered to portend madness or something dire happening to the brain— even though the vast majority of hallucinations have no such dark implications. There is great stigma here, and patients are often reluctant to admit to hallucinating, afraid that their friends and even their doctors will think they are losing their minds."

Sacks was writing about hallucinations in general, but those born of grief—of the garden, not traumatic, variety— have traditionally been given a pass in the mental illness classification system. In its most recent edition, however, the *Diagnostic and Statistical Manual of Mental Disorders* (DSM-5) has removed this exclusion because bereaved people could also be diagnosed with major depressive disorder. It was an acknowledgement that while grief and depression are different, they can co-exist. Post-bereavement hallucinations are listed in the DSM-5 as a subsection of "persistent complex bereavement disorder" and are described as "hallucinations of the deceased's presence." Critics worried that removing the exclusion would medicalize grief. In a 2015 literature review of PBHE, University of Milan researchers concluded that "given current uncertainty over the continuum of psychotic experiences in the general population, whether or not they should be considered pathological remains unclear."

Looking back, it's possible that my bereavement experience was complex. At the very least, it was layered and intensified by the factors surrounding my brother's death: his alcoholism, which may have been linked to mental illness; how impossibly young he was when he died from that addiction; and by the shame attached to his demise. People struggle with or battle other diseases, but such valiant language is rarely applied to the alcoholic whose body succumbs to self-abuse. My brother soldiered through the final stages of his life, and in his battle he lost a woman he loved, his creativity, his job, his connection to his family, and his shot at the regular humdrum existence those of us on the sidelines take for granted.

I don't know a lot about my brother's earliest years, but in family portraits he looks like a content, if wary, child. He was the third of four children from my father's first marriage, which lasted a little more than a decade. After the divorce, my two brothers remained with their mother, and my two sisters moved with our father to a nearby city where he'd been offered a job as a visual arts professor at the university. My mother, a young widow who was fifteen years my father's junior, entered their lives a few years later and another two years after that I was born. I remember this period in stories and photographs: My teenage sisters existed in a perpetual state of rage and blue eyeshadow, and we had a deranged dog named Buffer who snarled at paper boys and peed on visitors to our home. My brothers, not yet teenagers, visited on weekends. Like clowns, the seven of us would jam into the tiny family Renault for weekend outings to the local

Chinese restaurant or to comb the neighbourhood when the dog escaped, which he did with regularity. By the time I was seven my sisters had both married and left home, and my brothers' visits were less frequent. In that stiller, quieter life I became an only child with all the attention, privilege, stability, and opportunity that afforded. My life, I have always known, has been simpler than the lives of my siblings. My parents stayed together, I had very little competition for attention, and I did not grow up with an alcoholic mother.

My brother was a third-generation addict. I once interviewed a distant relative for a book I was writing, and she'd confused me for one of my siblings. "Your grandfather was a sensitive, kind, and compassionate man," she'd said. "But he was destroyed by drink." She was talking about my siblings' maternal grandfather—who was of no relation to me—but she might as well have been describing my brother.

Here is what I'd add: He had a yodel-like laugh; he was a skinny, anxious teenager who carried me on his shoulders; and later, he became an imposing figure to my high-school boyfriends, and an occasional confidante. In adulthood he was a talented artist who was a master draftsman and the responsible manager of a framing shop where he built beautiful frames of wood, gilt, and glass. Now, I know him best from the works of art he left behind—a linocut of two apples in shadow; a pen-and-ink sketch of a beat-up leather briefcase, open and empty; a miniature, remarkable self-portrait, done in pencil, yellowed from age and folded from being carried in his wallet, as if it were his driver's licence. These pieces of my brother's art hang on the walls of my parents' home, and sometimes when I visit I'll find myself gazing into one of them expecting something profound to reveal itself. Eventually, though, I'm always left staring at my own reflection in the glass.

*

My brother's funeral was on an unusually cold day in September 2001. We gathered at the cemetery at noon. Fat raindrops fell from the sky, and the mist cast a grey pall across the tombstones. There was a giant-size undertaker in black tails, arms outstretched as if he were gathering the rain from the sky, who waved the funeral procession toward him. Slow-moving cars snaked over the bumpy gravel road that cut through the graveyard. At the gravesite there was a black canopy erected over our heads and a stretch of burlap beneath us. I stood with my surviving siblings and my parents around a small rectangular hole, not much larger than a shoebox, that had been cut neatly from the earth at our feet. It was tiny, as if we were burying a dead bird we'd found in the yard rather than the cremated remains of my brother.

Afterward, we met in a church basement with grey indoor-outdoor carpet. People ate sandwiches held together by toothpicks and drank bitter coffee in Styrofoam cups. We were collectively damp from the rain. Wet overcoats hung in the corner, and we all had mud on the soles of our shoes. The women wore black dresses; the men, dark suits.

I stood in one corner of the basement holding a paper plate piled with food that I didn't touch. People lined up to speak with me, reintroducing themselves, some taking me into their arms. After offering condolences, my mother's cousin wandered into small talk. She asked me what street I lived on in Toronto. I swallowed and looked down. I opened my mouth, but I couldn't tell her. I breathed in, my heart raced, and blood rushed to my head. I felt like I might be sick. I couldn't recall my address. I could envision my front door and the adjacent park, but the street name, no matter how hard I tried, escaped me. "I just can't remember," I told her.

*

I had no control over when I'd walk past my dead brother in a crowded bar or see him on a bus, but I was the master of my waking dreams. In one fantasy, I invented a different outcome for my brother, while simultaneously reimagining my role in his life. In the imagined, impossible future I saw a Toronto coffee shop in winter with sun shafts sweeping low across a mottled wood floor. The tall windows were frosted, there were a few muffled coughs, and a quiet conversation drifted from the table behind where I was sitting. I was at an indiscriminate age, a random plot point on my future narrative. My oldest brother walked through the door, a bit late, to meet me. It was a casual rendezvous, something that happened on occasion but not quite weekly. He pulled the chair opposite, sat down, made a joke about the venue I'd chosen—it was a little gritty, a little bourgeois, elite but well worn. He called it "bohemian" and said it was reflective of who I was. (Of course it was! I'd scouted the location, lit the scene, chosen the interior decor, and hired the extras; this was my fantasy.)

Here is what he'd be doing: teaching at the art school in Toronto, living in a west end apartment not too far from a streetcar stop. He'd still have the printing press he left behind when he died, the one that lives in my dad's studio now. Or, scenario two: He left the framing shop he'd managed and opened his own, and he had a roster of local artists as clients, some of them my dad's friends and some new people in his life, younger clientele he'd found on his own. It's not unthinkable. He was organized, meticulous, and fiscally responsible—his careful life savings were a surprise to discover after he'd died. At thirty-five, he had enough cash saved to divide four ways—between his mother and her three remaining children. I declined my share. Not because I'm virtuous, but because I'm superstitious.

We reinvent our dead. We renovate their architecture, redecorate their interior, and refurnish their rooms. The alternative-future stories I dreamed for my brother changed with each telling, but one detail remained the same, because it had to, because without it none of the future life, imagined or real, would be possible: he was sober. Additionally, he was still making art. The two facets of who he was were intertwined. Without one, the other was impossible. Consumed by alcoholism, he was eventually no longer able to create art. Then, he died.

In the precarious and shaky time after my brother's death, when months accordioned into a single day, I shared this fantasy, truncated into a sentence, with my mother.

"Maybe if he'd checked into rehab, stayed sober, we'd have become friends? Meet for coffee?"

"It's possible," she'd responded, but she didn't sound convinced.

My mother is a novelist, and what I've observed is that although fiction writers work in the realm of the imagination, it doesn't mean they trade specifically in fantasy. The imagined world is rife with realism. If my brother was a character in a novel, would readers believe he could join a twelve-step program, conquer his addiction to alcohol, and change his life? We never had a casual meet-for-coffee relationship, so developing one in our later years was unlikely. You can't force camaraderie with people, even if they are family. Maybe especially if they are family.

I can imagine a brighter future for my brother, but there's a more likely outcome had he lived to see his fifty-sixth birthday this year: the bleak reality of a long-term addiction. Last winter I walked by a man vomiting onto the sidewalk outside a downtown sneaker shop, a bottle of whisky in his grasp. It was December, nearing midnight, and cold. I thought of my brother. I wondered where this man might sleep that night. I remembered how after my brother's funeral, my parents had gotten lost on their way from the service to the wake, and we'd driven slowly through a battered part of town where we saw two people staggering, ghostlike, along the sidewalk, their tattered clothes drenched by the earlier rain, their minds blotted by what—alcohol, or drugs—I don't know. "At least it didn't come to that," my mother half-whispered to my father in the front seat.

✳

That my brother was ranging around the city after his death might have had something to do with his life. In Scandinavian folklore there is a belief that the unsettled dead wander into the lives of the living. In some cases these represent the hug of the dead person, a concept similar to the idea of a soul. In other cases, they are revenants whose purpose is to haunt the known living. In one tale, a dead man seeks reconciliation with a neighbour he'd crossed, and in another a child haunts her parents because they'd forgotten to properly shroud her small corpse. The dead act as messengers, relaying the disaster of shipwrecks and the onset of storms, but sometimes they returned to offer basic life advice. "Don't sell," the dead mother advises when her son considers the fate of the family farm. In cases where the person committed suicide and their bodies could not be interred in sacred soil, the dead were forced to wander for the duration of what would have been their natural life.

The living, for their part, are more likely to experience visitations from their lost loved ones if the death was traumatic, sudden, unexpected, or untimely. This might explain why I have never seen my grandmother, who died peacefully at ninety-six, in the faces of passing nuns or in the eyes of blue-hairs at the bus stop. Tragedies, the personal, and in particular those on a mass scale, tend to breed ghosts, like those seen in post-tsunami Japan. A few months after the disaster, a taxi driver picked up a young woman near Ishinomaki station in Japan's Fukushima district. She asked the driver, a man in his fifties, to take her to Minamihama district, but he protested, telling her there was nothing left in that region.

"Have I died?" The woman asked.

The driver, stricken, turned to face his passenger, but she was gone and his cab was empty. This was one of seven cases of ghost passengers documented by Yuka Kudo, a sociology undergraduate at Tohoku Gakuin University. In her study she discovered that all of the ghosts were young people. "Young people feel strong chagrin [at their deaths] when they cannot meet the people they love," Kudo wrote. "As they want to convey their bitterness, they may have chosen taxis…as a medium to do so."

It's possible that my brother's hug was unsettled, or maybe, like the young tsunami ghosts, his visitations were a manifestation of disappointment. A more troubling thought is that my unresolved issues with his death were preventing my brother from fully exiting the realm of the living. In their international bestseller, On Grief and Grieving, David Kessler and Elisabeth Kübler-Ross write that "hauntings contain valuable clues, threads to be followed to their source. They represent some unfinished business in some cases and offer great comfort in others." Psychiatrist William Foster Matchett felt that seeing or interacting with the deceased could provide "an arena in which old conflicts and old relationships can be re-examined and perhaps mastered." It's possible, then, that seeing my brother, over and over, helped me to know him better than I had when he was alive. Also, seeing him allowed me to reconcile the grimmer aspects of his lonely life and death. I'd catch traces of him wandering freely about town, in the faces and bodies of ordinary people living recognizable, maybe even happy, lives. In its own strange way, this was comforting.

Most of the research on bereavement fantasies and hallucinations found that these experiences were pleasant, and helped mitigate pain, but there were exceptions. Apparitions of a lost child, for example, could be painful and destructive, as seen in a 2002 study published in Psychopathology that focused on two grieving mothers. One of the women, who'd lost her daughter to a heroin overdose, repeatedly heard her child calling to her for help: "Mama, mama, it's so cold." This was, understandably, unbearable. It's a story that echoes across time. In "The Power of Sorrow," a Swedish ballad recorded in the seventeenth century, a bereaved mother weeps in a green meadow as a parade of young children marches by. She seeks her son among them and, improbably, there he is. Dressed in white, his head hung low, the child is carrying a heavy jug in his hands. The mother asks why he isn't laughing and dancing like the other children, and her son says that his jug is filled with the mother's tears. He could not join his peers so long as his mother wept. A variation of this story dates back to the 1400s and appears in other parts of Scandinavia and Europe, and as "No. 78 (The

Unquiet Grave)" in the ballads collected by the British folklorist Francis James Child. One version, called "The Burial Shirt," is featured in the Grimms' collected tales. In this variant, a young boy dies and cannot sleep in his grave because his mother's tears continually soak his shirt. When he communicates this to his mother, her keening subsides. In Sudanese folklore, the creator, Ajok, returns a dead child to their grieving mother and in doing so enrages the child's father, causing him to murder his wife and child. As punishment, Ajok revokes any future offers of immortality, and death becomes a permanent state. The message is consistent across cultures and throughout time—the dead never truly return. Add this caveat: Avoid expressions of excessive grief, or, as I understood it, don't tell anyone about them.

There is one place where you are encouraged to emote in the modern world, and that is in the therapist's office. For a short time, when I returned to journalism school after my brother's death, I visited a grief counsellor. She had looked young to me, and she seemed nervous and unsure. She'd been dispatched to my university along with countless others following the September 11 terrorist attacks earlier that month. My brother's death arrived on the heels of a global trauma. His life burned out amidst the broader fire engulfing our world. It was the event that the people of my generation would remember forever: where they were standing when they heard, who told them, and how the fall light shone through tree branches, casting a web of shadows on the sidewalk below. I think he was still alive when it happened. These might have been the last images he saw—burning buildings and desperate people leaping to their deaths from skyscrapers.

I knew my brother died from esophageal varices caused by his alcoholism, which meant that a distended vein burst in his esophagus and caused him to hemorrhage. But I'd told the grief counsellor no one knew exactly when he had died, or what it had looked like, or even how long his body had been in his apartment. All of this uncertainty had led me to imagine my brother's death, dredging up scenes that were gruesome and unbearably sad. I hadn't shared these visions with anyone—not my family, or my boyfriend, or any of my friends.

The therapist suggested that I concentrate on a work of art when these thoughts entered my mind, pull up a piece from my catalogue of banked images based on years of studying art history. It would have the added bonus, she suggested, of connecting me to my artist brother. I tried imagining a grand art gallery—neoclassical, European, with shiny wooden floors and high, frescoed ceilings. I walked these halls in my mind, but when I came close to the most famous and beautiful works of art I saw turmoil and sadness. There's a distant sorrow in David's pale, sculpted eyes. There's always an impending shipwreck in Turner's storms. Art is grimmer, darker, and more psychically probing than it is decorative. I saw the grief counsellor only twice, and I never told her about my bereavement hallucinations. I'd been too afraid to hear her interpretation. Back then, staying silent felt like the safest choice.

All those years ago, I didn't have the tools that are available to me now. I was just beginning what would be a lifelong pursuit of knowledge—first as a journalist, then later as an academic. I've since learned to question our perceptions of reality. I've learned to interview sources about paranormal or magical events and respect them by not asking if their experience was true, instead asking them to describe what happened and why. From my present vantage, I now understand that my responses to my brother's death were normal. Short-term memory loss is common during acute grief. Seeing dead loved ones in the faces of the living is something that happens in cultures across the world, as seen in folk tales throughout time and in more recent rigorous scientific studies. Bereavement ravages your mind. Logic slips. You mourn your loss—the person you knew and the one you invented, and eventually, as the years pass, they fuse into the same being.

My brother's name was Marsh. It was his middle name, inspired by a family surname, but it was the only name his friends and family called him. Yes, I learned his first name after he died, but this no longer shames me. It never occurred to me that he was anybody but Marsh. Why would it? Still, a name is important. With a name you bestow meaning and history, or sometimes you like the shape of its written form, or the timbre of its syllables. You don't name in sorrow, or in an effort to shape or to mould. You name with possibilities, endless and passing. You name in love. So when my second and final child was born I placed Joseph between his first and last names. Its origins are Hebrew and, loosely interpreted, it means to give another son. It's got a beautiful cadence, and I chose it because it's a meaningful reminder of my brother—not of his death, but of the life he lived—and because I felt it deserved a second chance.

✳

It's now been twenty-one years since Marsh died, and I no longer encounter versions of him on the street. There is something inherently sad in the knowledge that I have, most likely, seen him for the last time. The sharp edges of this trauma have been blunted over the years, and I have stopped dwelling in my loss. I've also forgiven myself for not knowing my older brother. I missed him when he vanished, and now I believe that is enough. These are reasonable explanations for why I've stopped having grief hallucinations, but I have a parallel theory that runs closer to Scandinavian folk beliefs and tsunami ghost sightings in Japan: that my brother's soul, his hug, was unsettled for a time, maybe a decade or more, but that he has now found peace. Together, but on separate paths, we have both moved on.

Nuclear Folklore

PAUL EVANS MET ME AT the door of his home at 150 Dorset Street in Port Hope, Ontario. It was August 2016. Evans, silver-haired, seventy-one, a fast talker with a British accent, was wearing shorts and a collared shirt, as if I'd caught him en route to a country club tennis match. His wife, Helen, was charming on the phone, bubbly and warm. I'd called when I arrived in town and we agreed to meet at their house in ten minutes. But when I rang the bell only her husband and a small dog, the latter like a children's toy, answered the door. Evans showed me to a front-porch seating area, making it clear I wouldn't be going inside. He sat on a porch swing and I sat opposite him on a small couch. We were surrounded by soaring trees on the back half of his double lot, affording privacy from the neighbours whose century homes were set closer to the road, as had been my uncle's house, which had once stood on this same lot. It was a place I'd heard stories about since childhood.

I was visiting the Evanses' house to ask about the site's nuclear heritage, part of a story I'd spent the previous year uncovering, one connected to my family. During our one-hour meeting, Evans alternated between hostility and charm. He accused me of trying to ferret out information on the nuclear industry. He wouldn't tell me anything about his background, only that he was retired and that he moved to Port Hope ten years ago. Even simple questions were laced with tension.

"Where did you move from?" I asked him.

"We were refugees."

"From where?"

"Toronto."

I laughed. I thought he was making a joke.

"It's not funny," he said. He paused, then repeated himself. "It's not funny."

I stopped laughing. He was right. It wasn't funny. None of it was.

*

In the late fall of 1977, the Port Hope *Evening Guide* ran a front-page story about a radioactive century home that the Canadian government's Atomic Energy Control Board (AECB) paid to tear down. The address was 150 Dorset Street. The accompanying black-and-white image showed a post with a rectangular sign, about the size of a shoebox, and on it the trefoil symbol with its radiant petals. Behind the sign were the remains of a Victorian-era home: a set of front-porch steps leading nowhere, two decorative cedar trees standing on either side of its sagging handrails. A few steps further in, the roof's eave has collapsed into a pile of red bricks and splintered wood; planks from the home's hardwood floors, pieces of crown moulding, and the newels, spindles, and caps of the main staircase had all been reduced to rubble. The demolished home had been one of a cluster of stately residences along this west-end stretch of Dorset Street in Port Hope, a tidy Loyalist town with Canada's longest-running nuclear refinery at its core. The town is surrounded by a largely agrarian region, collectively known as Northumberland County. It's where my great-great-grandparents settled in the nineteenth century, escaping Ireland just before the famine. Their descendants lingered in the region and you can still see their surname on businesses and mailboxes throughout the county. My parents live there, and so do my aunt and uncle, and some of my mother's many cousins. Our family cottage is on Lake Ontario, thirty-five kilometres east of Port Hope.

In the three years leading up to the end of 150 Dorset Street, all homes in the town had been checked for radiological contamination, prompted by the discovery of radon gas in a local elementary school that had used free infill from the plant (then called Eldorado Nuclear). Similar issues cropped up in a subdivision built on toxic landfill and in homes where people had renovated using the refinery's architectural cast-offs (items such as old doors and floorboards). It was the largest nuclear cleanup in Canadian history and, over the next seven years, 200,000 tons of contaminated earth and homes were removed.

Two years into this investigation, on August 6, 1976, a gamma radiation survey of the property at 150 Dorset

Street showed elevated levels of radioactivity and the next month, on September 3, 1976, technicians returned to take radon air samples in the home. The results, along with an urgent memo, were sent to the AECB head office. Byron Boyer, an AECB official based in Port Hope, wrote to his superiors in Ottawa: "As you will note it is quite highly contaminated and probably should not be lived in until it is cleaned up." The letter is dated October 27, 1976. The letter notifying the owner, a single man named Robert Zeller, dated a month later, takes a calmer tone, explaining that further testing is needed because of "slightly higher" radiation levels.

The problems at 150 Dorset Street were unlike the other cases, in that they were much more severe. There was surface radiation in every room, meaning that someone who'd lived there had carried radium particles on their body; they'd left traces of it on doorknobs and walls and tracked it across the floors with their shoes. Hugh Spence, a public relations official for AECB, blamed outdated health and safety practices. He told a local reporter that in the 1940s when Eldorado Nuclear was refining radium—much of it destined for the Manhattan Project—employees must have worn contaminated clothing into the home. At that time, Spence said, 150 Dorset Street had been divided into apartments that housed employees from the plant. It was, in other words, a rooming house packed with careless technicians leaving a trail of nuclear breadcrumbs in their wake, the same material that fuelled history's largest deployed weapon of mass destruction.

Files show that the AECB pressured Zeller, the home-owner, not to speak with the press and, based on news-paper clippings from the time, he complied. That way, Spence could shape the arc of the narrative. He didn't relay that the levels of radioactivity in the home's seven fireplaces were staggering and that a glass jar containing radium bicarbonate had been lodged into a joist beneath the floorboards on the main level of the house, informa-tion I found in a previously classified AECB file. Over the course of a typical year, humans receive a dose of about 600 mR/hr of radiation from a combination of manmade and natural sources. A person spending six hours in the living room at 150 Dorset Street would receive the same dose.

Once surface radiation enters a person's body, via their skin or mouth, it stays there for life. The AECB knew it was important to test not just Zeller, who'd lived there for a year, but also the previous occupants of the house. The AECB claimed to be having trouble tracking them down, though from the time of contamination to discovery the home changed hands only three times. It was in 1970 that the house was sold in an estate sale to my uncle, John Carter, and his then-wife, Ilona Kirby. "It was the kind of house that you looked at and dreamed about owning," he told me. "God almighty, those houses were big up there."

Before the wrecking ball, 150 Dorset Street was a tall, ramshackle, red-brick Victorian beauty, trimmed in white with a wraparound porch that had begun to sag. It had a grand entrance with a sweeping curved staircase that reminded John of Twelve Oaks in *Gone with the Wind*.

Dorset Street runs along a ridge that sits about twelve metres above the lake, and from 150's front porch you could see the smokestacks of the nuclear refinery in the town's main harbour. Despite that, it was (and still is) a prestigious address, flanked by tony manors built in the last century.

After my uncle and his wife purchased 150 Dorset in 1970, they rented out space on the second floor to a high-school teacher in his mid-twenties named James Rose. Even still, the space felt cavernous and when John was away for work Ilona would sequester herself in the living room at night, closing the door to keep out drafts, lighting a fire and pulling her chair close to the hearth. "I would rest my feet on the edge of the mantle to warm them," she told me. "I got as close as I could." As sparks gave way to flames tiny flashes of greenish-blue light spread across the rear wall of the warming stone hearth, each about the size of a pinprick. They looked the way a night city appears from the window of an airplane. Ilona noticed this curious phenomenon every time she lit a fire. Years later, she recalled that the lights were odd and strangely beautiful, but not alarming.

Five years later, John and Ilona sold their rambling Victorian mansion to Robert Zeller and moved to a small town about forty kilometres east of Port Hope. Another year passed and for some reason Zeller stopped paying the mortgage, which he'd taken over from Ilona and which remained in her name. She considered taking legal action. Then, a phone call from a friend changed her mind. He was in Ottawa, working as the primary health physicist for the AECB. A troubling document had come across his desk. "You might want to hold off on pursuing that matter with the current home owner," he said to Ilona. "There's something you need to know about the house on Dorset Street."

A year later, in 1977, the home was gone, demolished, though if you look closely at the photo in the Port Hope *Evening Guide*, you can see that a listing brick chimney remained stubbornly erect. But that didn't last much longer, either. Before winter set in, it was removed, along with the rest of the debris, the two cedars, the ground cover of crisp fall leaves, and several feet of earth below the site. It was loaded onto trucks and transported to Chalk River, 180 kilometres northwest of Ottawa, home of the Waste Management Facility of Atomic Energy of Canada Limited, which is a stand-alone Crown Corporation (the AECB was replaced by the Canada Nuclear Safety Commission in 2000). There the remains of this once stately home will be stored for unknown centuries to come in sleek white containers designed to hold the vast amounts of nuclear waste that we still have not figured out how to deal with.

A couple of weeks after the demolition of 150 Dorset Street the first snows fell, quietly blanketing the now flat patch of ground. It was as if no one had ever lived there and nothing had ever happened.

✱

The first time I heard the story of my uncle's radioactive house was at our family's summer cottage, a blue clapboard saltbox on the shore of Lake Ontario in Northumberland County purchased in the 1930s by my grandparents and great-aunt and -uncle. Over the past six decades an open-pit limestone quarry swallowed most of the land directly west of us, reconfiguring the coastline in shape and matter; the water receded and what had been a stretch of sand became piles of palm-sized rocks.

I was about nine when my mother became leery of the lake. "Don't swallow!" she'd call from the shore. Afterwards she'd quickly usher me into the rickety tin shower. The 1987 Great Lakes Water Quality Agreement between Canada and the United States identified forty-three areas of severe environmental degradation (today, they are called "chemicals of emerging concern"). Our lake had seven such areas and two were nearby; sixty kilometres east in the Bay of Quinte and, of course, in Port Hope. The town drew special mention in the 1987 document due to the radiation contamination of Eldorado Nuclear's toxic legacy. An estimated 85,000 to 95,000 cubic metres of radioactive settlement had leached into the town's harbour since the company began operating in the 1930s. The refinery altered the chemistry of the water by its plant cooling practices, its shoreside dumping, and its misguided waste storage methods.

Port Hope is not alone. There are thirty nuclear-related facilities on Lake Ontario alone and the discharge drains of some of them empty directly into the lake. My children swim in Lake Ontario, but more troubling is that nine million people rely on it for drinking water. Nowhere else on this planet is freshwater used for drinking and as a nuclear cooling system. Since 1997, the monitoring of radionuclides (unstable isotopes that can emit radioactive gamma rays) in the lake has been spotty and they were not included as a chemical of emerging concern in the 2012 Great Lakes Quality Agreement. If you want your beach and water tested for radionuclides, you'll have to do it yourself.

My Uncle John is seventy-seven now. His hair is mostly grey. He remarried and has been with his wife for more than thirty years. She has two children from a previous relationship but John does not have children of his own. After four decades of practising law, he is now retired. At first, my uncle had seemed resistant to talk about 150 Dorset Street. When I visited my parents over an Easter weekend I'd peppered him with questions while my mother dressed the turkey. Finally he rubbed his temples and hung his head. "It was a long time ago, Emily," he said. "I'm surprised I remember as much as I do."

But the next day he dropped off a stack of documents. "Someone needs to find out the truth," he said. He'd kept two files on the incident, one full of basic realty information, the second more like a research file full of evidence you might gather to mount a case. Among yellowed newspaper clippings were my uncle's correspondences with the AECB requesting information on his former home, and asking that he and Ilona be tested for exposure to radioactivity. The second request was denied based on the health of Robert Zeller, who'd bought the house from John and Ilona, and who had passed the test. This is, of course, shaky science, since people have differing susceptibility to radiation exposure. Not to mention different lives—Zeller had only lived there two years, whereas John and Ilona and their tenant, James Rose, had lived there for five.

My uncle hadn't known James Rose well and struggled to remember much about him. There was a separate entrance to his apartment so their lives didn't often connect. Through archival files and by speaking with his best friend, I discovered that Rose was a bachelor who worked as a history teacher and was the basketball coach at Port Hope High School. He lived in town for less than a decade before moving to Mississauga, where the AECB reached him to have bloodwork done. The results were normal.

My uncle and Ilona did eventually get tested, thanks to John's badgering, and they both "passed." But the AECB continually denied John access to the radiological survey information on his former home. As with much of the information about the house on Dorset Street, John and Ilona had to rely on rumours and stories. The strangest of which turned out to be true.

*

The story I remembered from my childhood was that a mad scientist had stolen radioactive material from Eldorado Nuclear and conducted experiments in the fireplaces at 150 Dorset Street, after which he'd stored the results of his experiments in mason jars he hid under the floorboards. It turns out that Willem van den Belt was less a mad scientist and more of a jack of all trades: sailor, pilot, crocodile hunter, land surveyor, regent boy, refinery support worker, technician, black-market profiteer and, when he died at age sixty, he was running the woodworking shop at Lakefield College, an exclusive private boarding school in Port Hope. Van den Belt lived at 150 Dorset Street from 1942 to 1948 while employed at Eldorado Nuclear. He is both named in a *Globe and Mail* article and referenced in AECB files as the person who was responsible for contaminating the home. His goal, it seems, was not rogue science but something far more banal: profit. He was high-grading radium and refining it in the fireplaces with the aim of selling it on the black market. Back then, even trace amounts of radium were valuable. We don't know if he succeeded. William van den Belt, son of Willem, was interviewed in a 1977 article in the *Globe and Mail* and he claimed his father only distilled radium at work, but he did mention at least one curious incident. "I remember also that he had a platinum cover for some kind of container and he had a couple of little plastic bottles containing material that glowed," he said. "He himself was burned. I think whatever burned him had been spilled in a pocket of his coveralls."

By 1950, Van den Belt had moved on. Two decades later, Ilona was looking at blue-green sparks in the fireplace. There would have been no way to know that they were the remains of Van den Belt's DIY radium refinery.

Before you purchase a home in Port Hope today, most realtors will give you a copy of the site's radiological survey as part of the home inspection process. The final document on 150 Dorset Street in the AECB file, now the Canada Nuclear Safety Commission (CNSC), was dated 2013. It was a letter from the current owners: Paul and Helen Evans.

The CNSC had offered the Evans a radiological survey, but they'd politely declined, believing the levels wouldn't have changed since the previous year. "It was and is of no concern to us," they had written.

If there are any lasting effects from living in a radio-active home for five years, they haven't manifested in my uncle or his first wife Ilona. John is surprised that no government officials have ever offered to monitor his health. "We were the most obvious people for them to check out and follow, to this day, even. And they didn't; we had to contact them," John said. "Aren't they inter-ested in some scientific way, curiosity, something as to what might happen?"

Radiation exposure can have an effect on future gener-ations, as witnessed after the Chernobyl disaster. John and Ilona didn't have children together and neither one had children with their subsequent spouses. James Rose, their tenant, didn't have children either. He stayed a bachelor until he died, at fifty, the last of his family line. I know this because twenty years after 150 Dorset was demolished, in December 1997, my mother received a letter from his mother, Doreen Rose, who explained that she had read a story about my mother, who is a novelist, in a national magazine and recognized her as the sister of her son's former landlord. She was writing with a question that had plagued her for the past decade: "I have always wondered about the health of your brother and sister-in-law," she wrote. "I hope they are both well and haven't developed any cancer." Her son James had developed osteosarcoma—bone cancer—in 1990 and after seven operations it moved to his lungs. He died in 1993.

Timothy Jorgensen is the director of the Health Physics and Radiation Protection Program in the Department of Radiation Medicine at Georgetown University Medical Center and the author of *Strange Glow: The Story of Radiation.* I asked him if living at 150 Dorset might have killed James Rose. Based on the survey numbers from 150 Dorset, Jorgensen isn't convinced that's how Rose contracted cancer. "People who get cancer, they're always trying to find out a reason why," said Jorgenson. "Just like this guy's mother thought it must be the fact that he lived in that house. I think it's very easy to jump to that conclusion, but the fact of the matter is that cancer is a very common disease."

Exposure to nuclear radiation causes cell damage at a molecular level, and these mutations can lead to cancer. But it depends on the dose. Long-term exposure to low-level radioactivity near the refinery, which is now run by Saskatchewan-based Cameco, continues to be monitored. In April 2009, the CNSC published a report that synthesized all the environmental and epidemiological studies done in Port Hope and concluded that "no adverse health effects have occurred or are likely to occur in Port Hope, as a result of the operations of the nuclear industry in the community."

Despite this bureaucratically unsurprising reassurance, the notion that seemingly inanimate matter is alive, distilled with stardust from millennia-old explosions, and that this matter emits an odourless, invisible, tasteless gas that can interfere with the cells in our bodies is at once terrifying and abstract. And, with their hyperboloid cooling towers and black-and-yellow trefoil warnings, nuclear power plants can provoke anxiety in even the most level-minded who, influenced by images of previous catastrophes elsewhere, see the plants as looming disasters. The irrational (or warranted) fear of radiation exposure even has a name—radiophobia—and some experts believe this can be more dangerous and have a longer-lasting effect on your health than the toxin might. In other words, if the radiation doesn't kill you, the fear will.

For Ilona, the anxiety related to having lived at 150 Dorset was difficult. When I called her in 2016, we hadn't spoken in nearly thirty years, yet I found her voice unchanged and her memory sharp. She told me about meeting two nuclear industry officials, one sweet, the other surly, to discuss the contamination issue. She'd arrived feeling aggressive, but the kind man disarmed her. He asked if she had any children, and sighed with relief when she said no. The second man, with ham-fisted delivery, informed her that it could take up to twenty years for radon-related lung cancer to develop. Ilona is healthy and in her seventies now, but speaking about Dorset Street still rattles her. "I had dreams about that house for a long time," she told me. "Horrible dreams."

We live with radiation daily. If you are reading this in Canada or the United States, using indoor lighting, in a heated or air-conditioned office, in a public space, or in your home, you already have a relationship with nuclear power that you can't live without. This mythic-sized power can be destructive but it also allows us to live comfortably. There are nineteen nuclear power reactors in Canada, producing 15 percent of all of our electricity. The United States has ninety-nine reactors producing close to 20 percent of the country's electricity. Some might argue that nuclear energy also plays a role in saving the planet. Nuclear power emits far less CO_2s into the atmosphere than fossil fuels and is nearly on par with solar and wind power. But waste remains the most pressing issue, not just in our time, but for hundreds of thousands of years into the future. The white drums of Chalk River that house Canada's radioactive waste—including the remains of 150 Dorset Street—are mere stopgaps awaiting a permanent solution. There is talk of burying it deep underground. But, to date, no one has suggested a foolproof plan. Or found a volunteer host. It's not just an issue of what to do with the waste produced by the nuclear industry. It's an issue of how we're going to power our futures without continuing to poison ourselves.

*

I can't say why Helen Evans was not there when I arrived at 150 Dorset Street to talk to her and her husband, Paul. It had only been ten minutes since we'd spoken on the phone and she had asked me to come by. I wanted to ask them why they had declined a radon test when offered one by the CNSC. Helen never did materialize and Paul

Evans was animated and tense throughout. As Paul and I sat on their front porch, the swing creaked. He'd heard stories of long-ago technicians who wiped down their work areas and then smuggled the cloths home, burning them in the fireplaces of the original 150 Dorset Street to refine the radium, a mix of rumour and PR spin that has lasted nearly half a century.

He ran me through a quick history of 150 Dorset post-remediation: a local contractor bought the empty property in 1978 and moved a carriage house onto the site, taking it from a grand heritage home he'd been working on elsewhere. The contractor went "tits up" according to Evans and the project stalled for three winters until 1981 when a diminutive seventy-one-year-old named Hazel Horn stepped in and had the renovations finished, including a back kitchen extension. There had been plans for a large basement underneath the kitchen, but Horn didn't need this extra room. Her contractor hired a local construction business to fill and seal the extra space.

In 2003, nearing ninety, Horn moved into a retirement home and put the restored carriage house at 150 Dorset up for sale. Evans and his wife saw possibility. They bought it and began extensive renovations. As with all properties in Port Hope, they received the radiological history of their home in advance of the sale. It was colourful, certainly, but they were confident that the property had been remediated. Tests in 2003 had noted high radon levels, but a letter from an AECL representative explained that this was a result of the home being left vacant. At one level, it made sense. Radon is naturally present in most homes and can reach higher levels in places without airflow, like basements, or in buildings that have been sealed for a long time. However, that was not the case in the carriage house.

"It was a waffle weasel letter," Evans said.

In 2015, new cleanup efforts in the town had begun through an organization called the Port Hope Area Initiative. Much like in the 1970s, the initiative began to check homes for any lingering radioactivity. A survey of the land and gardens showed that the 1970s remediation efforts had been successful at 150 Dorset, but at 1,200 Becquerel per cubic metre (1,200 Bq/m3) of radon air, the interior of the carriage house told a different, and troubling, story. The World Health Organization pegs the acceptable radon air level at 100Bq/m3. The math is simple. Twelve times the limit. There was, once again, a problem at 150 Dorset Street and Evans knew immediately where it was.

"I told them, 'Look in the basement,'" Evans said. "They got down there and said, 'Oh, yes, this is slag from Eldorado Nuclear.'"

150 Dorset Street is, once again, radioactive.

"So having in 1977 cleaned up the site to pristine condition, AECL, through lax regulation, and I would maintain absolute negligence, allowed the local yokels to dump 200 tonnes of radioactive filth into the back kitchen," Evans said.

*

It's not human nature to leave the earth alone. We scratch, we dig, we gouge, we build. We form a task force to clean up our mess and then we start all over. Our grandchildren will one day die but the radioactive matter we've dredged out of the earth will not. In government literature, the contamination of Port Hope is referred to as an historical event. This is a misnomer. With nuclear waste, there is no such conclusiveness to be had.

I had parked at 150 Dorset Street so that the nose of my car faced the footprint of the original house. I'd hoped to take a photo, but Evans escorted me to my vehicle when I left, so I didn't. The meeting had been fraught. I didn't want to agitate him further. Mostly, I just wanted to get as far away as possible. There wouldn't be anything to see in a photograph anyway, just the empty space where a house once stood. There were hawks circling overhead. The cicadas were singing. Turning the other direction, I could see the lake stretching out to meet the horizon.

I thanked Evans. As we said goodbye, our pleasantries were punctuated by garbled vocal sounds from the tinny but audible intercom of the nearby Cameco plant. The sounds felt like distant, coded messages, or maybe they were just ordinary communications. The intercom went quiet. Then came one long, low whistle.

The Plague Legends

SHE WEARS A RED SKIRT. She is sometimes a goat. She is a hag. She is beautiful. She is two people: an old man and an old woman, or a boy and a girl. Her name, when she has a name, is Pesta.

She is the ferryman's passenger and he recognizes her face. He pleads for his life. He is a kind man. She can see this. She relents. She says: *I'll see what I can do.* She speaks in an upbeat, almost cheery voice. *You're probably not on my list anyhow.* She unfurls her scroll. She scans the names. She comes to a stop.

He is on her list.

Oh, I'm sorry, she says, and she is sincere. But her hands are tied. She lifts her staff, points it at the ferryman's heart. His heart stops beating. He falls. He is spared, not from death, but suffering. So that's something.

*

The scroll arrives on our doorstep on a Friday morning in March. Our neighbour, who is an artist, leaves it as a gift. In an email he writes that he hopes this ream of blank paper will give my husband and me something to do with our two children while we are sequestered inside because of the pandemic. On the first afternoon, my daughter cuts a long sheath from the scroll and claims a corner of the kitchen floor to work, as far away from me and her little brother as possible. My son paints a mural of the school where he attends kindergarten, which has been closed for five days now. There are eighty windows on its façade. (We count them, not from memory but from an image I find on the internet.) Now there are two schools in my home—one on the computer screen and one taking shape in the mural that my son is painting. There is a third, if you include the slapdash homeschool I am running in an effort to keep the children entertained. The third school mostly involves painting, and now, thanks to my neighbour's kindness, we will never run out of paper.

＊

If you see her approaching your village and she's carrying a rake, it's not good, but it's better than if she's carrying a broom. If she's carrying a broom, no one will survive.

＊

I number our days on a strip from the scroll, writing out what we will do with our endless spools of time. I write

in pencil and my daughter carefully copies over my words
with a thick black marker so she can see them. Once the
list is finished, these activities become a statement rather
than a suggestion and there are fewer arguments, but
not none. Yesterday, I found my son, his nose bloodied,
holding a fistful of his sister's white hair. I yell and my
husband yells. The children also yell. We howl like a pack
of wolves, and we are caged, all together.

If we are wolves, I think, then we will go to the woods. This
is on the scroll-schedule anyway. Every morning: Walk the
dog. It is a trick of the mind. We are the dogs.

We go early to avoid seeing other people. We travel single
file along a thin trail that cuts through unmarked bush
rather than walk on the wide paths in the adjacent city
park. Most mornings, we are alone. If we do pass another
human, the children leap into the tall grasses and hold
their breath. I think this may appear rude, but I don't
dissuade them. It's probably not a bad idea.

At night, in our attic, which was my office before the
university closed and it became my husband's lecture hall,
I research plague legends. These are mostly supernatural
stories inspired by the Black Death, which happened in
the fourteenth century and was the most fatal pandemic
in human history. The legends I read were collected in
Europe—although the internet can take me further afield,
to Russia or Japan, cholera or flu.

I have a small library of journal papers and collections of legends from when I was a graduate student in folklore. Legends are fragmentary narratives in which the action is immediate and presented as true. The characters are often nameless, with no backstory, and identified only by generalities such as occupation, gender, or age. Legends cross class divisions, cultures, and generations. They are spontaneous, with no formal structure, and are not exclusive to a storyteller's polished repertoire. Anyone can tell a legend.

Legends are nearly impossible to record in an organic setting and equally difficult to define, although some have tried. In 1958, Norwegian folklorist Reidar Thoralf Christiansen published a migratory legend index, a classification system that has been used by scholars to group legends by theme and subtype. Since so many of these stories appear in different parts of Europe and North America—they recur with similar motifs, differing only in their specifics of place—the legends are thought of as "migratory," as if travelling through geographies and across time of their own accord. Within this system of classification, a legend that incorporates supernatural elements and is told in the third person can be classified as a fabulate. This was once believed to be the truest, most poetic form of the genre.

The plague legends I seek out are bound by historical events and propelled by the collective fear of disease. But in form and function they are not unique from other narrative groupings. They also make use of the same motifs commonly present in other types of legends, such as spirits of the sea, or buried treasure, or—more contemporarily—food contamination, kidney thievery, or hitchhikers who vanish at night. I find four types of plague legends in the original migratory legend index, and eight more appended by folklorist and UC Berkeley professor of Danish literature and culture Timothy R. Tangherlini in the late 1980s. All are titled and numbered like the rest: "ML 7085: The plague ferried across a river," or "ML 7080b: Plague as a couple, young or old, with rake, shovel, broom and/or scythe."

You could call my research mythological doom scrolling: the grimmer the legend, the more sated I am. I go to bed only once I've read the worst, most appalling pestilence tale I can find. The news cycle does not offer what I need to hear about humanity, but legends are travellers, shapeshifters, easily following the path of disease and transforming to capture our fears and societal problems. They are the real story.

*

The gentleman is a messenger for the king. He travels across the kingdom leaving gifts on behalf of the crown—along the roads, in people's homes, and, curiously, in the water in their wells.

But the gift is not for everyone. The gentleman does not visit the kingdom's large cities, for instance. *There are too* many poor people living in the countryside, the king said to the gentleman before he embarked on his journey. *Disperse the cholera there.*

✳

The voice I heard while reading legends quietly to myself had, for a long time, sounded anonymous, placeless, and from a different time, a stiff recording by some long-gone folklorist playing in my inner ear. But lately, this is changing.

One night, I am walking with a friend along one of the empty streets of our neighbourhood. Her mother just called, she tells me, and worriedly relayed that pharmacies are running out of prescription drugs. Her mother insisted she'd heard this from a reliable source.

We continue on the road, six feet apart, looking over our shoulders for cars. We begin to swap other rumours, calling across the space that separates us. My husband's childhood friend suggested chewing zinc tablets. My friend's colleague is urging her workmates to buy winter boots for their children now, because supply chains are breaking down and they won't be available by fall. My sister heard—maybe from a friend, or from social media—that drinking warm water will flush the virus into your stomach, allowing it to bypass your lungs. My sister is now drinking small sips of warm water all day long. These are falsehoods, and, logically, I understand this. But the fear that propels the rumours is real, gnawing, and impossible to ignore.

Back home, I tell my husband the stories I learned while out roaming the neighbourhood with my friend. As I'm speaking, I remember from my studies that these are called FOAF (friend-of-a-friend) legends, tales that receive social validation through proximity to the source ("my sister heard ...."; "her colleague said ...."). I've come across these legends in my life before, but only occasionally. Never so many at once.

After that night, I begin to hear specific, modern voices when reading the plague legends. It's as if these ancient stories are now being told by my friend's colleague or her mother. I hear them in the voice of my sister, or of my husband's childhood friend.

*

When the ship beaches, there is no one aboard. No one alive, anyway; maybe the crew members remain in the vessel, but none have survived the journey. Because the ship is empty—or at least empty of the living—the villagers feel it is not a crime, moral or otherwise, to plunder it for its contents.

The villagers redecorate their homes with cargo: a captain's chair, an oil painting of some faraway bride, monogrammed silverware to fill their drawers. They eat for days from the ship's well-stocked larder. What good luck, they think, for these treasures to have arrived on our shores. Then, slowly, one by one, they begin to die.

＊

I am reading the same legends I studied as a graduate student ten years ago, but the stories are telling me something new and urgent. Legends can feel anonymous, as well as timeless and placeless, but they are often traceable to specific cultures and geographies. Some can even be ascribed to an individual—a storyteller who is sometimes named in a published text, although just as often they remain anonymous.

When small bits of personal information make their way into the narratives—a reference to an uncle or neighbour, a specific place name, use of the first person—the legends are classified as memorates. These stories were once considered the bycatch of legend scholarship, not true legends, like the fabulates. In the past, legend scholars went so far as to remove scraps of context found in the memorates. Today folklore scholarship largely accepts that these personal details are fundamental to the study of folk belief, and that individual stories are universal.

There is a third classification for legends, chronicate, which rarely turned up in my studies. These are personal narratives that are not supernatural and are considered to be based in fact. Chronicates are not easily categorized and, therefore, appear in the migratory legend index unnumbered.

By their nature, plague tales are collective and personal; the experience of a plague is both intimate and common. And though they often appear with supernatural elements, they are sometimes true. They are memorate, fabulate, and chronicate.

*

Two orphans dig a hole, as instructed. The villagers say: "You can have your lunch in the hole! Jump inside! It will be fun!"

The little boy and the little girl jump into the hole, sit down, and begin to eat.

"Why are you throwing dirt on my nice sandwich?" the little boy asks the man with the shovel.

*

She is the only woman left alive. She wanders from village to village but finds no one. Once, she finds a footprint. She bends, kisses the imprint in the sand.

*

The basement is musty and patches of dampness mottle the cement floor, so I sit on a blue plastic Ikea bag to eat the Easter chocolate I bought for the children. Both of them are upstairs looking for me. I stay quiet so they cannot find me, so they do not discover me eating the treats that should be theirs.

I risked contracting the virus by going to the local pharmacy to buy these crackly chocolates: therefore, I tell myself, I deserve them. (So far, in this sitting, I've had eight.) When I ventured out, I brought the surgical mask my father-in-law dropped off for me, but I sat in the parking lot for some time, deliberating about wearing it. I put it on, took it off, put it on again. Ultimately, wearing the mask made me feel like a criminal, so I left it in the car.

As I stood in line to pay, an older man, holding a white paper prescription bag in hand, was heading briskly toward the exit. His wife was several feet behind, jogging to keep up. "Not too close," She called after her husband. He ignored her, heading towards me as if with intention. I tried to move out of his way, but was trapped by a display of chocolate eggs and bunnies and chicks. I felt the wool of the man's coat against the back of my hand as he brushed by. His wife angled herself so that our bodies wouldn't touch as she squeezed through. "Sorry," she called over her shoulder before they slipped through the automatic sliding doors. I wished I'd worn that mask. I hardly heard the clerk at the checkout counter, but she had a sympathetic look in her eye. I bought so much candy that when

I got back to the car and looked at the bill, I wondered if the amount was a mistake.

While I eat the chocolate in the basement, I have dark thoughts. *Having two children was a bad life choice*, I think. *They do not play together. They torture each other. It would be easier to homeschool just one child.* Then I feel guilty. After a few more bites, I go upstairs and tell them I was doing laundry.

*

An officer in Japan's Higo province—Kumamoto Prefecture in present day—is sent to investigate a disturbance at sea, a green light on the water that seemingly has no source. His superiors would like to understand its origins, so, dutifully, he visits the shore to find out. There, aglow in the shallow water, he meets a charming woman who is half-fish and half-duck, and possibly also a mermaid with three tails. She is called Amabie, and she is prophetic. Starting now, she says, a plentiful harvest will continue for six years. At the same time, disease will spread throughout the country. To ward off illness, she says that people must draw her image and share it with others. You will need to draw me now, she adds, prompting the officer.

As she requests, he sketches her, carefully drawing her flowing hair, her diamond-shaped eyes, and the scales on her three tails. When he returns to the village, he shares his story as widely as he can. The villagers etch his drawing into woodblocks and publish it in the regional news—although most people only read the local bulletins for gossip and rumours. In this way, the story seems ephemeral, easily ignorable, but it endures. Whenever it is needed, even many generations later, the legend returns.

In our current pandemic the Amabie is

> a pastel pink Easter cookie
> a puff pastry
> a scarecrow
> on posters in the train station
> on Twitter, hitting her peak at 46,000 mentions a day
> a collage
> carved into a sausage with limp spaghetti for hair
> a costume
> the face of the government's contact tracing app
> felted
> painted
> global

✳

I unfurl a long piece of the scroll across the kitchen table and draw my best approximation of the Amabie. She has scales, a duck's bill, long hair, and three mermaid tails. The children help me paint her. We hang her on our front door to ward off the virus. My son is entertained, delighted by the strangeness of my behaviour and the new appendage to our home, but my daughter is on the cusp of finding me and my interests embarrassing and would prefer to hang a drawing of a rainbow in our window like everybody else. She asks that the Amabie stay on our door for only a few days. I'm not sure if this is enough time for the Amabie to do her job, but I honour my daughter's wishes.

*

A woman in white—tall, with messy hair—arrives in the middle of a party. She says that everyone in attendance will be punished for dancing the polka. No one sees the plague coming, even though they were warned.

*

We couldn't go to the public pool that summer. The playgrounds were closed. Our neighbour, who is nearly ninety, is leaning over her walker, telling me about a polio outbreak during her childhood in Toronto. *We couldn't play with other children. We stayed away from crowds. The beginning of the school year was delayed after summer vacation. We had to wait until October to go back. Parents taught their children at home.*

In a flash, so brief and fleeting that I nearly miss it, I hear a different voice, telling a similar story.

We had to teach our children ourselves. The playgrounds were closed. We washed our groceries, even the packages and tins. We left our mail and other delivery boxes in the basement for three days before we opened them. We were trapped inside for months, for years. We were scared.

The narrative is spare, an echo tale blurring what is personal and what is collective until it is difficult to recognize either. The story is a legend, and the voice is my own.

✳

I write to our artist neighbour and tell him about the Amabie: how we painted her on the paper from his scroll and she now hangs on our front door, which faces his front door.

Everyone needs their amulets, he writes back. *I'll look out for her.*

Days later, he writes again.

I'm clearing out my studio, and I have a bin of seashells, bits of wire, copper, and crystal from a chandelier. Might be fun for the kids to make sculptures with this stuff. Would you like it?

We would, I tell him, and the next day I discover a blue plastic tote on my porch. It is filled with shiny magenta Christmas balls, shells of all sizes, small pieces of framed glass with tiny flowers encased in them, copper spirals, ivory buttons, handfuls of beads, a mismatched pair of bulbous earrings made from seed pods, bits of wire, and a jam jar of chandelier crystals. Together, the children and I unpack the treasures, categorizing, as best we can, these disparate, magical items. We work methodically, deliberately slowing down time, making something from these fragments of the past—something beautiful, something surprising, something entirely new.

✳

The girl is the only person left alive in her southern village. She climbs the mountain and calls out across the valley. There is a boy—the last of his village, too—who lives on the northern slope of the mountain. He hollers back in response. They find each other, marry, and have many children. They leave behind two place names: Call, in the south, and Answer, in the north.

✳

I fold our painting of the Amabie into a manila envelope. With it, I stash one of our weekly schedules, my son's mural of his school, and eighty printed pages of stories that I recorded from our lockdown spring. I write *Time Capsule* across the envelope in black marker and tuck it into the attic storage space where we keep our camping gear, extra blankets, and boxes of old photographs.

It will lie there, untouched, when the mask mandates come into place, when the children return to school in the fall, and when the school closes again in winter. It will remain, unchanged, when the virus mutates and becomes more infectious, when the first vaccines are approved, and when large groups of people refuse to take them. It will be there, largely forgotten, when the schools reopen yet again the next year, and when my two children walk there together, without me, for the first time.

As I stand watching them walk away, I will not think about the time capsule. I will watch as my daughter loops her arm protectively over her little brother's shoulders and wonder if the enforced intimacy of the lockdowns changed their relationship, or if they would have grown this close regardless. Deep in the attic the time capsule will persist, inert, untouched, until some distant point in the future when my children discover this archive of fear and ordinariness. Just as there is hope embedded in the very existence of the plague legends, which continue beyond their own times, one day my children will unfold the artifacts of this time and understand that they have survived, and that they have a story to tell.

Adrift

THE PEOPLE BEGIN TO ARRIVE on Saturday morning. They drive down the lane of the cottage next door and park their cars on an angle to accommodate as many vehicles as possible in the small spot of grass between the building and the forest. One driver is confused and speeds down our cottage lane at such a clip that I have to stand in his path, hold up my hands, and yell, "Stop!" He is looking at a map or a phone, and it is his companion who alerts him to my presence. The driver looks startled, and as our eyes meet he mirrors my actions by lifting his hands, palms facing out, before placing them back on the wheel and reversing his car up the lane.

The cottage next door had belonged to my aunt and uncle for nearly thirty years, and before that, to my great-aunt and -uncle for another twenty. Then, last August, my aunt and uncle sold the cottage to two sisters from Ajax, a large suburb east of Toronto. The sisters are industrious. They painted the formerly yellow exterior white with green trim and the interior walls red. They threw away the antique family furniture my uncle had left behind and replaced it with new, store-bought items, like a leather armchair and a freshly veneered kitchen table with four matching chairs. Finally, they planted a garden, thick with pink roses and blue hydrangeas, that lined the perimeter of the cottage. On either side of the door, they hung baskets, dripping with fuchsia to attract humming-birds. After the sale, my family put up a fence between the two properties. The sisters even improved on this, plant-ing miniature conifers trees at each post.

My uncle's former cottage is a square bungalow with two bedrooms and an adjoining, open-plan kitchen and living room. The front façade faces the lane, and the back, which has a long narrow porch, faces the water. There is a small lawn that ends at a moderate cliff, and below this is the rock beach which sometimes stretches six feet to the shore and sometimes is non-existent depending on the whims of Lake Ontario. Both inside and out, it is a small cottage for a party.

It is early June, the mornings are still cool, and the frigid lake water will be un-swimmable for another month. In a regular year the children would still be in school, my husband, Andrew, would be going, physically, to work every day, and we would not be here yet. But this hasn't been a regular year. The global pandemic arrived in winter and despite watching parts of Asia and Europe lock down to quell the spread of the virus and understand-ing the gravity of these situations, it was nevertheless surprising and disorienting when our two children came home from school for March Break and never returned.

*

Earlier on Saturday morning, before the people began to arrive, the older sister's son stopped by his mother's cottage. His name is Michael and I would guess that he is in his mid-twenties. He was unstrapping a kayak from the roof of his car. I was chasing my dog, who was sitting on the front stoop of the cottage next door, expectantly wagging his tail, hoping to be let inside. We'd tried to curtail this behaviour, but dogs have long memories.

I apologized to Michael. I want the dog to stop making these forays next door, in part because of the social interactions it inevitably provokes, which are friendly, but, after the third or fourth time it happens in a day, a little forced. No doubt it's awkward for the neighbours to have me repeatedly turning up on their lawn. I began to tell Michael that my uncle used to feed the dog and this is why he is so persistent, but he cut me off.

"Yes, I know, he used to feed him," he said.

He gave me a funny look and maybe I imagined this, but it seemed as if he shook his head, slightly, as if in exasperation. I ignored his response, pushed on, cajoling the dog, asking Michael if he was planning to go kayaking that day. He said he wasn't, that he was just dropping the boat off and that a few people would be arriving later in the morning. When the dog ventured close enough to me, I grabbed his collar and dragged him home. I turned to wave over my shoulder to Michael but he'd disappeared into the cottage.

*

I watch the people next door with lurid curiosity. Who are they? Where did they come from? Why are they so brazenly breaking the gathering limit rules? My parents live five minutes from our cottage but, following public health guidelines, we do not enter their home when we visit. The people next door are hugging each other and laughing, open-mouthed, and coming in and out of the small enclosed space of the cottage, and presumably they will all sleep there together, too. They have set up a propane stove on the small lawn and have gathered folding chairs in a circle around it, sitting so closely their shoulders touch.

I don't feel lonely. I am never alone anymore. But I yearn for the ease of a party, having the pressures of entertaining, feeding, cleaning, of conversation shared among many. I envy the neighbours' freedom, their lack of fear, so at odds with my own experience of trying to harness this threat, of drawing inward, of helplessness. My feelings about the gathering next door are more psychological puzzle than moralistic judgment. It hadn't occurred to me that life could carry on as it had before. It has only been a few months since the onset of the pandemic, but I had believed that humans had been rewired, our behaviour fundamentally changed from what it once was. Now, I see that while the consequences might be different—illness, possible hospitalization, passing the virus to someone vulnerable—socializing looks the same.

*

Around noon, a woman from the party next door appears on our lawn. Andrew is in the back cabin, working. The children are eating lunch in the screened-in porch: macaroni and cheese with heaps of ketchup. I step outside to greet the woman, who has bangs and long red hair, and who introduces herself as Nhi. Every time she steps towards me I step back.

"My friend is on the lake in a boat, and we can barely see him anymore," Nhi says.

I glance toward the horizon and squint. I don't see anything.

"Is he in a kayak?"

"No." She shakes her head and looks confused. "It's a white, um, rowboat maybe?"

"Oh, right," I say. I know this boat. It had belonged to my uncle. He left all his belongings when he moved. This boat is forty years old and made of Styrofoam. It has a low hull, and once had a sail and a rudder but now has neither.

"When did he leave?"

"He's been gone two hours."

"Does he have a phone?"

"No."

"Does he have a paddle?"

"It is short, and broken, but yes, he has a paddle."

"Can he swim?"

"He is okay at swimming," she says, then pauses to further consider the question. "He can maybe swim in a pool."

"Is he wearing a life jacket?"

"No."

I see a brief mental image of the missing man clinging to the hull of the overturned Styrofoam boat, his only means of staying above water. I take a breath, look out at the lake, then back at Nhi.

"Wait," I tell her. "I'm going to call a neighbour."

I call Frances, who lives in the big blue house at the foot of the lane that leads to the five cottages in our bay. She is in her seventies and used to run a bed and breakfast out of her home until her husband died unexpectedly one spring and she abruptly shut down the entire operation. Frances has had to ask for emergency help in the past, as her guests often found themselves in trouble on the water. Once, two men visiting from the city had tried to windsurf on the lake in winter and had become trapped by the ice shield that had formed along the shore. The waves had repeatedly smashed the windsurfers against the ice, breaking their bones and dragging them beneath the crusted surface before spitting them back out. The rescue had been difficult, but they were eventually pulled out along with their broken windsurfing boards.

"He won't survive in the water if he capsizes," Frances says. "It's too cold."

"I know," I whisper, turning away from Nhi. She is growing increasingly anxious, alternately staring at the lake, then back at me, standing in place on our lawn.

"Tell her to call the police right now," Frances says.

I relay this information to Nhi. She nods, but she does not turn to leave. The children have finished their lunch, and through the porch window I can see the table where their two empty bowls sit smeared with cheese and ketchup. They are now playing on the tire swing a few feet from where we are standing, eavesdropping. My son waves to Nhi. She waves back.

"Could you call the police?" Nhi asks me. "I don't even know where I am."

My son turns to me, his eyes wide. He tries to speak but his sister shushes him. *Not now*, she hisses, in a voice that sounds very much like my own.

I've been coming here all of my life, as my mother had, and as her mother had. Right now, I am the only person able to give directions to our location, to name the bay, the beach, the roads, the place names, and the number of our laneway. Not even Andrew knows these details.

I call 911 while standing with Nhi, trying to keep the recommended distance from her, while also acting as a medium between her and the police. The officer, or dispatch person, or whoever is on the other end of the phone, asks me the missing man's name, and I ask Nhi.

"It is Truong Nguyen," Nhi tells me. She spells his name for me.

"His age?" I ask her, parroting the person on the phone.

"Maybe thirty-four or thirty-five?"

I can tell that she's guessing. Why doesn't she know? Maybe he's a new boyfriend? Are people still dating during the pandemic? How do they meet? How did these two end up here together? These are not, obviously, pertinent questions for this situation, and I don't ask, but I do wonder.

After hanging up, I call my mother and tell her not to visit today. She will not like what is happening at the beach. She has developed a distrust of the lake. She feels its waves are targeted, that the undertow holds grudges. I don't know why her feelings for the lake have turned. She has been swimming in it for her entire life. She immediately calls her brother.

"Oh God, not *that* boat," my uncle says when my mother tells him that a man has gone missing. "No one should be in *that* boat."

✳

Andrew appears from the back cabin where he's been working. He grabs his birding binoculars and is able to tell Nhi that he can see her friend, but barely. He is a speck of white in the grey-blue water. The wind is blowing offshore. What is happening in the middle of the lake is harder to know. Are the waves larger, are there white-caps? Or could it possibly be calmer than on shore?

A six-foot person can see about three miles until the curvature of the earth will drop the horizon from view. Andrew, who is just over six feet tall, is unable to see Truong through the binoculars anymore. He has disappeared over the curvature of the earth. I find this difficult to comprehend when Andrew tells me this, as if it were an old-fashioned thing that people believed once, just as they believed the earth was flat, but he is a scientist and so I accept this fact. The other possibility is that Truong has capsized and we cannot see him because both he and the boat are under water. The first theory is the better option. The police are not here. It has been twenty-five minutes since I called them.

✳

Now it is half past noon, and Andrew is dressed in a hooded wetsuit. He is going to venture into the water on the stand-up paddleboard to save the missing man. Andrew wears a hat, sunglasses, and a life jacket. He tells me that he will be okay because he has sunscreen, water, and his phone encased in a plastic bag in his backpack. Until now, he believed the man in the boat would be fine, but, since losing sight of him through the binoculars, he is no longer certain the man will survive until the police arrive. If the police arrive, I think, because at this point I am beginning to fear they never will.

Nhi turns to the children, who are still on the tire swing but now openly watching the action, and she offers them ice cream. My son is elated, but my daughter, who is paranoid and rattled by the pandemic, turns to me, fearfully, as if the woman has offered her poison.

"Thank you," I say to Nhi. "But we are not sharing food right now."

Life has been consistently monotonous over the past few months. I spend time in familiar places with people I know well. Spontaneous interactions with strangers are brief and rare. They are never sustained, never ongoing. This morning, a man decided to launch an old boat and the wind direction changed. I didn't want to get involved with the people next door, but now we are connected in a way I couldn't have foreseen.

"I'm sorry, I hope you understand," I say to Nhi. I feel genuine remorse. I think it would have eased her nerves somewhat to distribute this small pleasure to the children. My son begins to cry about the ice cream. His sister hisses at him, again. This time I can't hear what she says, but it sounds mean.

Nhi brightens at the idea of Andrew using the paddle-board to save her friend, but I feel differently. I don't think it's a good idea. It has been the coldest spring on record. I worry that Andrew will end up in the water. A lifetime ago I was a teenage lifeguard, so I'm aware that unless you know how to approach them, a drowning person will drag you down with them. I also worry that if he does reach the missing man, he will contract the virus. I protest, but quietly, so the children can't hear and become afraid, and so Nhi can't hear me dissuading the rescue effort, although I suspect she's intuited that I don't want to let Andrew go.

He goes anyway, and is about twenty feet from shore when I hear the sirens. My son catches the faint wail and cocks his head like a dog and his sister nervously takes his hand, pinning him in place. I jump onto the beach and call to Andrew, waving my hands above my head, and then make exaggerated gestures toward the road.

"Stop!" I call to him. "They're here!"

Then, I run. I remember, also from my long-ago life-guard training, that someone has to meet the emergency response attendants and show them where to go. My phone rings and I hold it to my ear as I jog toward the sirens. It is a man from the Department of National Defence, which is located at the nearby army base. He sounds exactly as you might imagine a marine rescue dispatcher would—calm, unflappable, and serious, but in no way alarmed. He says, "Call us if those guys put a boat in the water."

"What guys?"

"The fire and rescue folks."

I briefly wonder why these guys don't speak to each other, and why this is my job. I am feeling as if I have too many jobs. Andrew is maybe still in the water? Where are my children? Are they still on the swing? What are they doing right now? Has my son accepted ice cream from Nhi in my absence? I promise to do as the man says and then I forget the entire conversation.

There is a fire truck at the end of the lane. The engine is running and there are other sirens approaching so the firefighter can't hear me. To get his attention, I grab his forearm, and then I remember that I am not meant to touch anyone but the people I live with. He is the first non-immediate family member that I have touched since I hugged my sister-in-law goodbye after she stopped by in mid-March to pick up a play kitchen that my son had outgrown. That night the province locked down and I haven't seen her in person since. The fireman says that they will assess the situation from the public access point, which is down past Frances's place. A police car pulls into the shared lane and the officer rolls down his window. I direct him to our cottage. "It's the blue one," I tell him.

✳

When I return, Nhi and the police officer are standing together on our lawn. My son is inching slowly toward the parked police car, which the officer has left running. The firemen do not launch a boat. Instead we see the red Search and Rescue Zodiac, heading east.

We stand on the lawn looking toward the horizon: me, Nhi, the police officer, who is weirdly silent and testy and not forthcoming with information about the rescue, my children, in the shade of the tree, and Andrew, returned from the water, still wearing his strange hooded wetsuit. I am wearing an oversized floppy hat that makes me suddenly self-conscious, as if it is too outlandish for the seriousness of the situation.

Two men from the party next door have joined us. I recognize one of them as the man who'd driven down our lane that morning. I notice that Frances and her neighbour Tom are standing on the beach, also looking at the water. All together we watch the red Zodiac speed towards nothing that we can see, and then we watch as it veers away from where we'd last seen the man floating and heads south. I worry that they are heading the wrong way and will never find him.

Nhi turns to me, questioningly, but I have no answers for her. I just don't have that information, and I can't guess. It reminds me of the relationships I form with new mothers of children who have the same genetic condition as my daughter. We are essentially strangers and they want so much from me, a level of clairvoyance I cannot offer them. They want to know exactly how their children see, what it means to be blind, but it's different for everyone. None of my answers, my examples of how my daughter lives and sees, satisfies them. But what do they see? they ask me, wanting an exact description of shapes and distances and colours and I don't have that information so I always end up disappointing them in some way although I am trying to do the opposite. With Nhi, who is also a stranger, I feel the same. I want to help, and I have more information than anyone else surrounding her at the moment, but I'll never be able to give her the answer to her question, which is: Will her friend survive? Because I don't know.

*

What is Truong thinking about when he is floating in the Styrofoam boat under the noonday sun? When does he know that his efforts to get back are futile, that for every inch forward he paddles, the current will push him back a mile? Does he instinctively know to be still, to distribute his weight so the shallow boat doesn't tip? Or is this something he learns during his time on the water? We've all been alone in our homes for thirteen weeks, and yet it strikes me that in the vast lake, the shore distant, if even visible, this man is more isolated than anyone else, even at this time of great remoteness. He has only the birds, the fish, the water, my uncle's boat, and a broken paddle.

I imagine that he hears the rescue boat before he sees it and, maybe knowing that he will be saved, he relaxes, leans too far toward one side, and this is why the boat capsizes and he falls into the water. Or maybe it is the Zodiac's wake that overturns the little boat. Still, it seems strange. The rescuers should know how to approach a vessel in peril without tipping it into the water. Just as I know that you must approach a drowning person feet-first or they will drag you under the water with them. And so, maybe it's not entirely an accident that the rescuers' boat tips Truong into the water. Maybe it's a lesson.

We will never know the inner thoughts of the rescuers, just as we will never know Truong's thoughts, as he drifted, further and further until the shore disappeared and all he could see was water.

*

"They've got him," the police officer says to Nhi. "They're taking him to the Wicklow Beach boat launch."

"He is safe?"

"Yep," he says. The officer is ruddy-faced and stoic. He does not elaborate and he does not say goodbye when he walks to his car, which is still idling loudly. He also does not acknowledge my son, who sits on the grass, hopefully, opposite the driver's-side door.

We are happy and relieved, me and Nhi. We smile at each other and breathe long sighs of relief. She returns next door.

My phone rings again. It is another police officer. He has a nicer tone than the officer who'd stood quietly on our lawn during the rescue. He says, "You better come and get this guy. He's struggling to communicate."

"Is he okay?"

"Oh, yeah. He's okay, but he needs a translator."

I write down the directions to the boat launch on a piece of paper that I take next door. There are tall plumes of smoke rising from the propane stove and I can smell cooking meat. The people sitting on the camping chairs turn to look at me; some smile. I hand the sheet with my directions on it to Nhi and explain the situation. The two men who'd joined us on the lawn say they will pick up their friend and bring him back. They all say thank you, over and over, and I feel embarrassed but also useful in a way that I haven't for some time. Of course, I'm useful in my domestic sphere, making meals, running a homeschool, keeping my children alive, but in the world beyond that I've basically disappeared.

*

Why hadn't the first officer told Nhi that she would need to pick up Truong from the boat launch? I think he is tired of people from the city, people like us, and like Nhi and her many friends. The city people come here to play, and then they need to be saved. They don't understand the water, they drown in it, they smash their bones apart windsurfing in Lake Ontario in winter—in winter! And now, they bring the goddamned virus with them. "I don't want those city people bringing their cooties here," the grocery store owner tells my mother, and I make sure to bring all of my own food when I visit.

The officer sees me and Nhi as part of the same group, and yet, earlier in the day I had assiduously avoided eye contact with the people at the party next door. *What does it matter if I ignore them?* I'd thought. They were just visitors, short-term renters. They would be gone by Sunday night, and so I believed they were inconsequential. The lines we draw around ourselves to the exclusion of others are infinitely changeable and equally arbitrary.

The police officer's disdain gives me the same feeling as Michael's head shake earlier in the day, but for different reasons. The police officer feels I am infringing on his territory and I make Michael feel as if *he* is infringing on mine. Michael is tired of hearing how the property, which legally and rightfully belongs to his mother and aunt, once belonged to my uncle, and that even our dog refuses to believe this place—the beach, the shoreline, the little cottage next door—could belong to anyone but us.

*

The water is glassy and still on Sunday morning, reflecting a cloudless sky. It is a different lake from yesterday, less anxious, less fraught. I am sitting in a big plastic chair on the beach reading a novel and the two women at its centre are, at the moment, all that I care about, although I'm attuned to any sound of waking children—a creaking door hinge, footsteps in the grass. When they see me here, they will want me to do things for them. The silence and solitude will be broken for the day.

I see a flicker of movement next door. A man, alone, smoking a cigarette, shifts in his lawn chair. He is not one of the two men I met during the rescue. I am now on friendly terms with them, strangers before yesterday, strangers still in a way because I do not know their names. This man, however, the one smoking on the chair, quietly watching the water, I know his name. It is Truong Nguyen.

We don't acknowledge one another, but I occasionally break from my novel to watch him. This is easy to do because my chair is angled slightly toward the cottage next door so that the rising sun lights my page. He stands up, stamps out his cigarette, and walks over to where my uncle's old boat is propped against a tree. Truong tips the boat towards him, grabs the gunwale, and lifts the vessel slightly off the ground.

I can't look away. It seems as if he plans to carry the boat to the shore, to launch it into the water. *Surely he wouldn't do that,* I think. *And if he does? What do I do?*

But he doesn't. He tips the boat back to where it had been resting, and taps the hull twice, the hollow sound drifting down the beach. Then he climbs the porch steps and disappears into the cottage.

*

I didn't expect to see Nhi and Truong again, but what is surprising is that I never saw Michael again, either. The sisters sold the cottage in August. They'd owned it for just under a year. People were paying outrageous sums for cottages that summer because everyone wanted to escape the city during the pandemic. This is the rumour we heard about why the sisters decided to sell, although all that painting and planting and updating suggested to me that this might have been the plan all along, the pandemic real estate spike being simply an added bonus. It was also possible that after the boat incident the sisters decided that renting the cottage was too onerous, liability being a real and constant fear. How can you be sure that a man staying at your rental house won't go missing on Lake Ontario in a rudderless boat with a broken paddle? You can't. If there's one thing I've learned since March, it's that people will do whatever they want, and often they will make bad choices and there's nothing you can do to control that. That said, the older sister, who always struck me as a take-charge kind of person, did ensure that no one could sail the Styrofoam boat again. She didn't throw it in the Dumpster as she'd done with my uncle's old furniture. Instead, she painted it gold with a green trim, filled the hull with earth, and planted a garden of red geraniums inside. So far, the new owners have kept Truong's boat just as the older sister left it. The flowers bloomed right into fall.

Years Thought Days

MY FATHER WAS IN HIS eighties when he fell in love, for the second time, with a woman he'd known in high school. Her name was Mary. On a morning in mid-July, he'd sat down with my mother, to whom he'd been married for forty-three years, and he confided in her. He was astonished, he said, that at this stage in his life he could feel this way. He was awed by the power of his emotions. That the rush of young love might return to him, now, when he was eighty-six, seemed remarkable. It was a kind of magic. He raised his brows, his eyes open wide. He shook his head slowly in disbelief.

My parents sat side by side on the loveseat in their living room while my father explained the situation with Mary. He apologized, also, for what this meant for his relationship with my mother. No one was more surprised than him, he told her, and he was also feeling very sad. It was clear that he was confounded by this sorrow, but what was more unsettling for him was the other feeling, deep like a cut, arriving unannounced at this late hour. *I just can't believe it*, he said to my mother, repeating himself. *At this age.*

By then, my father was five years into his official dementia diagnosis and Mary had been dead for a decade. Also, he had always been a faithful and loyal husband. Gently, my mother communicated the news of Mary's death to my father, but he either didn't believe her or promptly forgot the information. For the rest of the moment—for emotional events are fleeting for those with memory loss—he talked about his love for Mary.

My parents visited me that afternoon. I met their car in the laneway of our family cottage where I had been staying with my husband and two children for several weeks. My husband was working and the children were in the back cabin listening to an audiobook, or maybe fighting with each other. They were usually doing one or the other that summer, trapped as they were, together, with no chance of seeing another child on the horizon. Their parents and grandparents were the only alternative to one another, and parents and grandparents quickly lose their sheen. They preferred, instead, to listen to their books and to argue.

My mother handed me a white plastic bag of groceries she'd bought from the nearby vegetable stand. The bag was bulging with butter tarts and cheese curds, a quart of strawberries and a tub of vanilla ice cream for the children.

"Well," she announced. "Your father has rekindled his feelings for his high-school girlfriend."

My father stood beside her. He wore a straw hat perched atop his white hair, and a short-sleeved button-down shirt tucked into tan slacks. He has looked just like this for twenty years. Maybe more. It was strange, but he had not really aged over the past few decades. My father caught my eye. He shrugged and winked at me. He was smiling, cheerful, and he made no attempt to deny my mother's claim.

My mother's tone was without judgment, without accusation, or exasperation. She was amused, just as my father also seemed amused. Months later, when my mother and I spoke about the morning my father fell in love with Mary, she wondered how she might have reacted if it had been true. She wondered how she'd feel if Mary had been alive, and my father did not have dementia and its accompanying hallucinations, and he really had fallen in love with Mary again, as he had in his teen years. My mother said she might have reacted the same way. After all those years together, she told me, you know a person. She said she would have relayed a similar sentiment as she had that morning. She would have told my father that he might feel this way right now, but that it would pass. She would have said, *Let's get on with the day*.

*

This is what she had said to him that morning. Let's get on with the day. And they had. My mother had helped my father into the car and they'd driven to the vegetable stand and then they'd headed south to the lake where we stood now, together.

"I've never heard about Mary before," I said, mostly to my mother, but, at the last minute, remembering also to turn to address my father. He had stopped inserting himself into conversations by then. He listened, quietly, and you could forget to include him. I tried to avoid doing this, and mostly succeeded, but when I caught myself forgetting him, as if he were slowly disappearing, a transparency in our midst, I felt a terrible, crushing sadness from which I will likely never recover and never forgive myself.

"Well, she was your father's first girlfriend," my mother said. "Or, maybe, a kind of high-school crush? Anyhow, she was a nice woman, and we saw her occasionally when we visited Niagara Falls."

"Is she still alive?" I asked, and then I regretted having said this out loud. Or at least saying it in front of my father.

"Well, no, I mean, honestly, she'd be as old as him," my mother said, gesturing at my father.

It was possible that my father had discovered something tangible that had prompted this memory of Mary, maybe a letter, or an old photograph. He often rummaged through the drawers in his office, searching for what, we were never sure. Occasionally he did discover pieces of his past—unearthing old drawings he'd made as a teenager, family photos, business letters from art dealers who were now retired. Sometimes he would add notes to these artifacts, annotations that conveyed a sense of importance, or urgency, but were impossible for any of us to decipher. This didn't feel unusual. My father is an artist, and many of the marks he's left on the world are open to interpretation, from his abstract oil paintings and his three-dimensional landscape sculptures to his realist drawings of invented vegetation.

The more likely scenario was that my father connected with Mary through a memory. He had reached through the recesses of his saved past, through time, coming across places and meeting people he'd known, all of this personal history becoming fainter for him, more difficult to grasp, and he'd caught hold of a memory of Mary, from when they'd both attended high school in Niagara Falls, when he'd loved her, which was the first time he'd loved anyone in that way. He must have tripped here, remembering the complicated emotions of young love, a new state of being that also feels as if it has existed alive inside of you all along, before you yourself have entirely formed, so that you discover the force of yearning for another is twinned with the revelation, in yourself, that this force exists.

As I stood on the lawn with my parents, before we would go inside and have our lunch of butter tarts and cheese curds and ice cream, something in the back seat of my parents' car caught my attention. It was a pair of lurid red heart-shaped sunglasses. They lay shiny and still, illuminated in a sunspot.

"Whose sunglasses are those?"

My mother leaned over and looked through the window of the car.

"God, I don't know," she said, waving her hand as if the thought of these sunglasses tired her.

"What do you mean you don't know?" I often found items like this in my own car, but this made sense because I had two children. No one ever rode in the back of my parents' car, as far as I knew, and particularly that summer as it was still early in the pandemic.

"Well, what can I say? I don't know how they got there."

I narrowed my eyes and shook my head. The sun was getting hot. I heard the coo of a mourning dove from the nearby wood. I did not believe that heart-shaped sunglasses could turn up in the back seat of your only car without your knowledge. Someone must have put them there, but who? Was it possible that one of my children had found these glasses and covertly placed them there? And where would they have procured these glasses, anyhow? The kids were essentially trapped here by the lake. They hadn't been to a store in months.

My mother turned to my father, suddenly, as if she'd solved a mystery that had been plaguing the two of them for some time. "What do you think?" she said to my father, her face alight. "Do they belong to Mary?"

∗

There is a possible third scenario regarding my father's encounter with Mary, how she might have visited, then left her red heart-shaped sunglasses behind. It had something to do with my father's studio, where he made his sculptures and oil paintings. The studio is a small room at the back of the house. It is also where the recycling is kept and so whenever I carry an empty bottle or can or old newspaper to the bins I stop to look at my father's tools and at his art.

Last week, I'd noticed that my father's most recent oil painting was propped on a small easel on his desk, which was littered with tubes of paint, brushes, and oil sticks, as well as the tubs of modelling clay, Polyfilla, and crackle paste he used to create relief in his two-dimensional works. The painting was in a pinkish frame he'd coloured himself and was about two by three feet large. It was an abstract image of what seemed to be a dark and magical wood. There was a storm roiling in the navy-grey sky, a heavy wind blowing through yellow-pink branches, and whorls of blue leaves. Below, in the foreground, was the black mouth of a cave. This was a gate, a threshold between one place and another, an archway through which you would find yourself in an entirely different state of being. It was, I felt certain, the entrance to the otherworld. Could this be how Mary got in? Was this where my father wandered when he slipped quietly away into his mind?

∗

Mary didn't return to my father for the rest of the summer, at least not that he shared with us. He moved on and remembered, often vividly, other parts of his life, such as the architecture of his childhood home and its dark, handmade furniture, art shows that had taken place in the past or that were set to take place in an imagined future. He asked after his granny and his Scottish nurse-maid, Effie, who'd cared for him into his teen years. He made plans with his first art dealer, Av Isaacs, who'd been dead for some time, and he spoke often about his younger brother, David, as if he'd just returned from spending the afternoon with him, although David had died nearly a decade before.

Dementia is characterized by forgetting but it's also a long period of remembering, a return, it seemed, of people and ideas that have been important to you over your lifetime, as with the arrival of Mary on that summer morning. Although, of course, it was my father or, rather, his mind making the journey to meet the people of the past. He was travelling to them.

I could never accompany my father on the visits he took to the otherworld and could only imagine these places and meetings as described by him. I wanted to understand his desire to visit these imagined pasts, and, sometimes futures, and also, what prompted the visits, why they happened at all. In researching this phenomenon, I found a letter written by three scholars of gerontology and published in the *Journal of Psychogeriatrics*. The authors drew a parallel between a well-known Japanese folk tale, "Urashima Taro," and the experience of dementia.

✳

In this story, a fisherman named Urashima Taro takes a ride with a sea turtle to an underwater kingdom called Ryuga where he spends three days with a beautiful queen. The walls of her palace are a shimmery enamel and they are encrusted with coral. Life there is festive and Urashima Taro is distracted by the constant celebration. He finds himself caught in a loop of joy. He stays with the queen for three days and in nearly all versions of the story they fall in love. He leaves only because he pines for his elderly mother and frets that she might be worried about him. The queen protests his departure, but relents and gives him a protective gift. It is a box made of shells and gems and light which, she tells him, he must open only in a moment of extreme duress.

After Urashima Taro surfaces he's struck by changes in the landscape that he cannot explain. The grassy mountain slope where he lived had become densely forested in his three-day absence. In some versions of this story the forested slope had been logged and was now grassy. Either way, the countryside had dramatically shifted. Unsettled, he approaches an elderly man on the shore. He does not ask this man about the trees on the mountain. Instead, he asks about himself. He wonders if the old man has heard of a person named Urashima Taro. The old man nods, says that yes, he's heard of Urashima Taro, but not for a long time. He remembers him as a character in a story his grandmother told him. It is story about a man who went to live with the queen in the underwater kingdom. This man's family waited for him, but he never came home.

This happened three hundred years ago, the old man said, the way that one speaks of myths and folk tales and legends. They take place in a long-ago time which means they may or may not be true. Urashima Taro senses catastrophe, and, in desperation, he opens the intricate little box that the queen had gifted him. A thin line of smoke rises from the box and disperses into the sky. The smoke extinguishes the magic—it kills both the spell and the story. In an instant, Urashima Taro grows old, dies, and turns to dust.

In their paper, the scholars likened Urashima Taro's visit to the dragon kingdom to the journeys that people with dementia take into the past or into hallucinated scenarios and suggested that these delusional experiences are often pleasant while the realities of old age can be unpleasant. They wrote that "such a picture of paradise is unrealistic, but would be possible due to disturbance in orientation."

I didn't believe that my father was struggling in reality and happy only in delusion, and I wondered if it was possible to draw a line between these states for someone with dementia. It seemed to me that the two were paired and that hallucinations and reality happened at the same time. Nevertheless, something in this interpretation took hold and I could not stop thinking about what it meant. I kept returning to the concept of time, and how it compressed and expanded for Urashima Taro, for my father, and, to some extent, for all of us.

Time, as we experience it in the human world, is also a kind of magic. It can fly and it can stand still depending on our emotions. As we age it can speed up and in moments of peril it can slow down so that each minute that passes can seem an eternity. Time is as much a human construct as fairy tales. The sun rises and sets to bookend our days and carries us through the changing seasons, and the moon more or less creates months, but seconds, minutes, hours, and even weeks are up to our own discretion, determined by our cultural beliefs, set by the governments in the countries where we live, and beholden to the whistle of the approaching train, which, to be functional, must arrive and depart at structured periods of the day.

This might help explain why time doesn't exist in our memories. "Neuropsychologists have not been able to locate a mechanism in the brain that registers the time of an experience," writes Stefan Klein in *The Secret Pulse of Time: Making Sense of Life's Scarcest Commodity*. Further, he writes that the human brain has no marker for time. When we rummage through our remembered pasts, we register places, colours, emotions, sounds, and smells, but we do not have time stamps. We construct time, not the other way around, no matter how we may feel ruled by its power, and we do this through our experiences. "It is memory that creates the peculiar, elastic properties of time," writes Claudia Hammond in *Time Warped: Unlocking the Mysteries of Time Perception*. When memory fails, time becomes irrelevant.

*

In the early weeks of the first spring lockdown, my father was unable to hold on to the idea of the pandemic. He could accept it when the details were communicated, but he would forget again in a few hours, sometimes minutes, and, other times, in the very moment that he was being told. With every telling, he learned anew, adjusted, caught up in an instant to what we had lived for many weeks. He time-travelled like this every day.

One afternoon in early April I was speaking to my father on the telephone while my children watched a science show on television that I felt might pass as a homeschooling activity. I was lying on my bed, facing the window. I could see a parcel of overcast sky and a branch from the maple tree that grows on the boulevard in front of our house. There were several ragged brown leaves clinging to the branch and they were moving gently with the wind. This was my view, but I was conjuring a different landscape for my father in an effort to avoid speaking about the pandemic.

"Dad?"

"Yes?"

"I was just thinking about Lisbon."

"Oh, okay. What about it?"

"We were there a little over a year ago."

"Who was there?"

"Me, and Andrew and the kids, just for a week," I said.

I told him about how the streets were mostly made of marble. My son was four at the time, and had fallen constantly, often crying and demanding to be carried.

"It was like walking on a skating rink," I said.

My dad laughed.

"Where was this, again?"

I said, once more, that we'd been to Lisbon last year, and then I spoke about how the city is built on a series of hills and surrounded by water. I told him that we had stayed in Alfama, the old town, where the streets were made of cobblestone and were too narrow for a car to pass. These roads had been a terrible challenge for my daughter, who was eight at the time, and who has low vision. She should have been using her cane, I said, but she forgot it at home.

Then, I told my father about how my son rang the doorbell of an apartment in the building where we were renting an Airbnb, and how an old woman had answered the door. She was wearing a red and blue apron and her grey hair was swept into a tight bun. Her face was round and, I felt, open, ready, as if she'd been expecting us. I was embarrassed and apologized for my son, but she bent down and cupped his chin in her palm, and she smiled at him, and spoke directly into his little upturned face. Her tone was sweet although her words were lost on both of us. She straightened, finally, and she smiled at me and waved to my daughter, who waved back, and she spoke again in a warm, encouraging tone, and if I had to guess what she was saying it would've been that children are curious, and this is okay, so it's not necessary to apologize. This is what I had wanted to hear, in any case. I had invented her words and they had been a comfort.

"Imagine being that old woman living in an apartment in Lisbon," I said to my dad. "All those people from around the world traipsing up and down the stairs of your building." I conjured this now, too: foreigners pulling their luggage behind them, bumping their overstuffed duffel bags and hard-shell wheeled suitcases along the stone steps, still others with towering backpacks strapped to their shoulders. Then, I imagined myself as the old woman, hearing my doorbell ring, and opening the door to find a small Canadian boy wearing a blue sunhat standing in my entryway, a little boy with bruised knees from falling on the marble streets, a little boy who was unable to control his impulses when faced with a button.

"Yes, imagine that," my father said, and then he said, "Ha!" for emphasis. He spoke next, telling me about a spring he'd spent in Lisbon. I had known that he'd visited the city, but not that he'd stayed for a season. He was a young man at the time, not yet thirty, and he'd lived there with his first wife and my two older half-sisters, who were two and five at the time. He'd spent his days walking the city, stopping for several hours in various places to draw what interested him—a seaside vista, a gothic arch, a crack in the wall that had begun to germinate—and visiting the city's art galleries. My oldest sister went to an elementary school near their rental apartment. Sometimes my father would pass by the playground and stop to wave at her.

"You know what?" I said. "I'm remembering a photograph of Allyson wearing a grey pinafore." Closing my eyes, turning away from the window, the gauzy light, the branches against the sky, I could envision my older sister as a small child, standing on a playground, her sandy blond hair cut short, smiling at the camera, the children in the background a collective grey blur.

"You were so young then," my dad said.

"Yes," I said. "I was young then."

But the truth was that I hadn't been born yet. I wouldn't arrive for another twelve years. Also, my father had not lived in Lisbon, although I would learn this later. He was perhaps conflating a visit to Lisbon with a period of time when he'd lived in Spain with my sisters and his former wife. Or maybe he was imagining a different scenario, and I had filled in the gaps with what I remembered from family stories.

A few hours after I'd spoken with my father that April afternoon, my mother left me a voice message. "Well, your father thinks that you're in Corsica," she said. "He told me you called from there to say hello, and that you were happy. So, there's that. It's kind of nice at a time like this, isn't it?"

Listening to my mother's message, I thought of lying in my bedroom and speaking with my father, of looking up at the beige ceiling, and the crack that runs along it like a spine, and then, I saw something else, just beyond, a mirage of places past. Lisbon with two young children in tow—twin memories, my own and my father's, half a century apart. And, on the periphery, I saw the Mediterranean island of Corsica. It was just a shimmer, not a real memory. I've only ever been there in my father's imagination.

*

The unintentional false reporting of a memory is called confabulation. A memory maligner invents memories for secondary gain, but a confabulator makes up the stories of their past and believes them to be true. To some extent, we are all confabulators. Every time we retrieve a memory we change it just slightly so that the most treasured scenes from our past are the most distorted. Confabulation is a hallmark of Alzheimer's Disease and other forms of dementia where the warping of autobiographical memory occurs. It is necessary for people with memory loss to invent stories in order to communicate. It is a bridge, a boat, a means of crossing the water. Corsica is the mythical island my father visited in order to tell my mother the story of our conversation.

*

In August, about a month after we'd discovered Mary's heart-shaped sunglasses, I was sitting in the screened-in porch at the family cottage with my two parents. My mother sat to my left and my father sat at the head of the table, where he had a view of the lake, and where he has always sat. It was dusk, there was a small pile of dishes from dinner stacked at the other end of the table, a reprieve before dessert. The children were racing along the rocky shoreline, occasionally shrieking. They were throwing stones into the lake, rippling the evening's still water. A haze had settled on the water and there was no discernable horizon, blurring the lake and sky as if they were one entity. I could hear the neighbour's dog barking, the whir of a distant lawn mower. My mother was talking, winding up to her point, which I cannot now remember, and she had stopped, mid-sentence, because my father had a question. He didn't speak his question aloud; it was that a look of bafflement had crossed his face, as if he was trying to solve an equation or a puzzle. It was the kind of look he had when examining his drawings-in-progress, which were always pinned to a corkboard opposite where he took his meals. The corkboard in the cottage porch was on the wall behind my mother, but he wasn't looking at the drawings there, which were fading now, having over-wintered in the glare of the harsh, leafless light, and there had been no recent additions this summer. He looked at my mother, and then at me, and then he looked back to my mother again.

"What?" she'd asked him. "What is it?"

"Well," he said, looking at me again, then back to my mother. "I'm just wondering what the relationship is between the two of you."

This had happened to my mother before. My father had forgotten her, or questioned their relationship, or had asked my mother where his wife was when my mother happened to be standing in front of him, and so this was not an unusual situation for either of them.

For me, this marked the first instance where my father did not know me, or, at least, the first time he'd made this clear. I had feared this, suspected it was happening, once or twice, when I caught my father searching my face, not unlike he'd been doing that night. I felt that the first time my father failed to recognize me, a cavern would open in the earth beneath my feet and swallow me. I would live in the cavern, then, going forward. If my father didn't know me I would also cease to know myself, or to exist. I hoped the children would stay on the beach. I did not want an audience at that moment. I could tell by the sounds of their voices that they were drawing nearer to the cottage, circling the adults, hoping for ice cream.

My mother turned to me.

"Well?"

I took a breath and I pointed to myself and said, "Daughter." Then I pointed to my mother and said, "Mother."

I turned, then, to face my dad.

"You are the father."

I said this last part tentatively because I worried it might upset my father to learn such important information, or to learn that he had been unaware that he was seated at a dinner table with his wife and his youngest child. This was not what happened. Instead, my father's face lit up, as if this was a wonderful surprise, as if this conveyance of information was coming to him for the first time, and it was a true illumination, a pure and singular thrill. He broke into a wide smile.

"No wonder I'm having such a wonderful time," he said.

In that moment I learned an important and often overlooked feature of dementia: in forgetting there is also the opportunity for revelation.

*

Memory is ephemeral. The fragments that make up our days are easily forgotten. While I remember the sounds of my children playing by the shore, my father's smile, how the haze hung over the lake, other moments from that evening have fallen away and are now irretrievable. Hammond writes that "when we talk about the study of memory, really, it should be the study of forgetting. Every day we experience hundreds of moments that we simply forget." Memories can be lost as soon as they are made. Eventually, we will forget everything.

*

I hadn't known the story of Urashima Taro before reading the article in the gerontology journal, but I was familiar with a similar tale from Irish mythology. The protagonist, Oisín, follows a magical horse into Tír na nóg, the land of eternal youth, where he meets Queen Niamh and falls in love with her. In some versions he meets Niamh in the human world and she guides him to her home. He spends what he believes is a year in this land but he pines for his family, his brothers in particular, and, also, his house. Niamh tries to dissuade Oisín from returning home. She worries she'll never see him again, but she lends him her horse and sends him off with a warning: Do not dismount. Whatever you do, don't let your feet touch the earth.

Oisín returns to find his home in ruins, the stones barely visible in the tangle of vegetation that has grown in his absence. He learns that his brothers are long dead and that three hundred years have passed. Among the ruins he spots the remains of the old stone washbasin where his family had cleaned themselves, and he remembers being a boy and the sensation of water on his face, and he is overcome with the urge to touch the stone basin, now cracked and fuzzed in moss. He dismounts, and when he steps to the earth he ages immediately, and, just as Urashima had, he turns to dust.

In the Folktale Motif Index, a six-volume catalogue of the granular elements of folk tales, Urashima Taro and Oisín in Tír na nóg are classified under the heading Years Thought Days. The title refers to the supernatural passage of time that happens when a mortal makes a visit to the otherworld. The Tale Type Index, a companion to the motif index, lists hundreds of magic world stories that span the globe. In one, the otherworld is a hellish farmer's field where the souls of the dead are represented by thin or fat sheep, in another it is an island where you can only laugh. It can be a place inhabited solely by women or crocodiles or elephants or fairies or gnomes. It can be underwater, or in the sky, or in a bank of clouds the sun cannot penetrate. It can be a land of people with topsy-turvy morals, and it can be a world where houses are thatched with the wings of birds. The otherworld is malleable and changeable, subject to the whims of the teller and their culture.

Despite its many iterations, there are several rules that apply to nearly all the Years Thought Days tales. The first, and foremost, is that time passes differently in the otherworld than in the human world. The second is that you cannot travel through time by natural means; some space-time compression is necessary. The third is that the enchantment is limited to a specific time span, such as one year, seven years, or seven hundred years, and that this supernatural time span has a corresponding human time span. For example, three years in fairyland is equal to one human year, while three months in the underwater kingdom is akin to three hundred human years. A general rule of folk tales is that the storyteller must not describe the slow passage of time, what Danish folklorist Bengt Holbek described as "the slow change, the long and weary journey." This, in itself, is an act of magic, as a story that unfolds over an hour can traverse several generations.

Finally, while this is not a rule as much as it is a trend, these stories tend to have dystopic endings, which is unusual in wonder tales. Is Urashima Taro a sad story? I have discovered several versions since first encountering it in the journal article and I'm left feeling melancholic after each reading. It is a tale about the fleeting passage of time, how years can be thought days, and this is the central magic, but as with so many fairy tales it is also the central sorrow. In both the Japanese and the Irish tale, the hero dies in the end. At the heart of these enchanted stories lies the human world's ultimate truth, which is that nothing can change the fact of death.

*

I was standing in the threshold of the doorway that led from the formal living room to my father's drawing room, the room where he made art, but which had recently become his sick room, and where I believed he lay dying. He had been in bed for a few hours by then, in the new bed, the one that had been delivered in anticipation of my father's return from his stay in the hospital. I'd come to check on my father because I was afraid that he was trying to die, and if my mother and I didn't check on him often, that he might die alone.

It was dark in the drawing room, although some light filtered in from the living room, which has many table lamps, all of them aglow. In the dimness I could discern some familiar shapes, such as the long bookcase of paperback books, which were mostly biographies of artists, the towering shelves of records, the record player. I could make out the built-in bookcases that reached the ceiling, tightly packed with art catalogues and travel guides to Europe, where my father had travelled every year to draw and visit art galleries, museums, and churches. I could faintly make out the boxy hump in the corner, which was my father's piano, and, then, in the fading light of the winter afternoon, I could see his work desk by the north window, which was scattered with drawings-in-progress, pens and pencils, small watercolour brushes, postcards of artworks he admired, pots of ink, and thick pieces of handmade paper, all of this left as if he had been working and had paused for lunch, with every intention of returning after finishing his meal.

Last week, there had been a fall in the night from which my father could not right himself, and my mother had been unable to pull him up and so had called for an ambulance. When the vehicle pulled into the driveway, the red lights had illuminated my father's drawing room, where he had fallen, en route to the bathroom. The emergency responders were gentle and thorough and had discovered that my father had a fever, so instead of sending him back to bed they'd whisked him away to the hospital, a twenty-minute drive through the country. And then, days later, he was discharged with no diagnosis, no explanation, and no kindness. His body was stiff, and he couldn't walk unassisted. It took three people to get him into the car and yet, on the other end, there was only my mother to help him back out again and into the house.

I'd asked her how she'd managed this, but she said that she didn't know. It had been, we both agreed, some act of supernatural strength. I'd arrived an hour later to find my father inert, sitting in a chair by the fire, his chin resting heavily on his chest, his eyes closed. He was wearing a tan cardigan, corduroy pants, and a blue turtleneck that seemed to be on backwards. He looked distinguished, as always, but somehow smaller and childlike. I knelt beside him, and I held his hand, which was still but warm. I told him that I was there. I said hello, but it came out like a question: "Hi Dad?" The coronavirus numbers had been rising lately and so I wore a facemask, although who was protecting whom I could not begin to decipher at that point—I had children in school, and he'd been in contact with the various hospital and paramedic personnel. I was worried he wouldn't recognize me under my mask, but I heard him whisper my name. This is how I knew he was there.

In the late afternoon, my mother and I had helped my father to his bed. We supported his weight as he shuffled, inch by inch, across the kitchen, the dining room, the living room, and finally to his bedside. This might have taken twenty minutes or it might have taken two hours. I can't remember. Tipping him into his bed was difficult and terrifying. His body could not bend to sit, he could not lift his legs, he could not roll or shift, and although later I would learn there are techniques to help an immobile person into a bed, at the time I was only afraid. Afraid I would hurt him, that he would fall and we would never get him back up again, afraid that if we called the ambulance they would send him back to the hospital where it had been clear there was no place for him because the weekend was coming, and weekends, the head nurse had said, were busy. The act of helping him into bed also took a length of time I cannot remember or even guess at. I can say, only, that it was growing dark.

Hours later, as I stood at the threshold of my father's drawing room, I found his bed empty, the duvet thrown off, the impression of his body still in the white sheets. Because of the state in which we'd placed him in his bed, his complete inability to move, I believed, in that moment, that he must have vanished. I did not think that he had died, but that, instead, he had physically disappeared, that his body had lifted from the bed of its own accord, had been drawn up through the ceiling, and through the room above, the one with the two beds where I slept as a little girl when this house belonged to my grandparents, my grandmother in the bed closest to the window, then up through the ceiling of that room and into the attic which was crowded with my grand-mother's hardcover books about the great war, boxes of papers that had once been important, and leaning stacks of art, and he floated, then, through the roof and into the night sky and through the stars and the Milky Way and into the nothingness of the universe where he would be weightless and free and formless and this was where he would be, both nowhere and everywhere, but not in this bed, in this room, in this house.

Then, a movement in the corner caught my eye, and in the dimness, I could make out my father's figure, still wearing the blue turtleneck, moving gradually around the edges of the room. One of my father's favourite adjectives is "trepidatious" and this is how I would describe his passage through the dark. It was a slow and cautious movement. Although I could see my father, right there, in front of me, I still couldn't believe it was him, because it seemed so impossible to me that he would be upright. This magical thinking seemed a more likely conclusion than the mundane, simple, reality that my father had lifted himself from bed and wandered halfway across the room. Put another way, it was easier for me to believe that he had vaporized than that he was able to rise and walk.

Time was sliding back and forth and so I can't say how long I stood there looking at my father's imprint in the empty bed as he stood, in the shadows, looking at me. Had he also seen himself lifted through the ceilings, through the attic, into the night sky, the stars, and beyond? He never told me so. For that moment my father had existed in a parallel world, he had disappeared, and he was unreachable. He was not dead but he was gone and I could not follow him. He would not die that day, but the sense of losing him had wormed its way into my brain, as if it were a real memory, as if he had floated away into the universe and I couldn't quite convince myself, although logically I understood otherwise, that this hadn't actually happened.

*

It is impossible to know what gave rise to the supernatural time narratives. In her article "Spaces of Passage into Supernatural," folklorist Mirjam Mencej surveyed several theories on what might have inspired the stories of mortals journeying into the otherworld. One scholar writes that they were born of drug-induced hallucination, another that they were reflections of dreams or trances, and still another believed sleep and meditation inspired the theme of compressed time in these tales. Ultimately, Mencej writes, it isn't possible to trace their origins, and, instead, what connects these different narratives beyond the motif of the supernatural passage of time are the places in which these passages to the otherworld are located—water, woods, mountains, the mouth of a cave.

The article by the gerontologists is the only instance I could find where dementia was cited as a possible inspiration for such tales, but experts have drawn parallels between time travel and the experience of memory loss and have applied this to models of care. One example is a long-term care home in San Diego called Glenner Town Square that is a perfect recreation of a 1950s small town. There is a theory that our strongest memories are formed from ages 18 to 32 and so this village was for people who'd been born around the middle of the last century. The problem was that sometimes there was a mismatch. Some residents might have had urban backgrounds that didn't suit the more rural makeup of the fabricated village. Other residents might have been born slightly later and were now trapped in a time they had never lived through. Still others might be condemned to exist in a period they'd prefer to forget. This model has had some positive success, but research found that people with dementia had stronger and more positive reactions to their personal memories than a collective sense of place in time.

*

I was sitting on a small black folding chair at one of the three banquet tables that had been set up outside the long-term care home where my father now lived, waiting for him to appear around the corner with my mother. He'd moved here shortly after his fall last December. In the months following his discharge from the hospital, he hadn't fully recovered, had remained stiff, with his mobility greatly reduced. He'd often forget this, however, and would rise eagerly from bed only to fall again. He'd needed a new level of attention, and, at the care home, over the winter and into the spring he'd slowly improved to the point where he was, once again, fully mobile. He'd come back from his deteriorated state more or less the same as he'd been before. This type of recovery was unusual—new residents in care homes tend to decline—but, as one of his nurses said, it does happen sometimes. My mother was able to visit four times a week, but the home's stringent public health policies coupled with capricious government directives meant no other family member was allowed inside. This lasted five months and it was painful. My mind found it difficult to process that I was barred access to my father. Sometimes I'd forget about the rules and wonder why I hadn't seen him in so long. In these moments of distraction a terrible sense of loss would settle over me. I would remind myself that I was not allowed to see my father, but this only heightened my feelings of helplessness. I kept asking myself, but why are we doing this? I was never able to find a satisfying answer. A headline for a *New York Times* story about pandemic-era long-term care came close: "We are going to keep you safe, even if we kill your spirit." This was a quote from a doctor interviewed in the story and was in reference to residents. It could be extended to their families, however, on the other side of the door, never being allowed inside.

Today, I was still not able to go inside, to see my father's room, but, for thirty minutes, we could sit opposite one another, divided by a layer of clear plastic. Our table was situated around the building's corner, affording us the most privacy. From here we could not see the other residents with their visitors. A personal support worker in blue nursing scrubs stood beside me as I waited, and when she saw my parents rounding the corner, my father in a white dress shirt, my mother all in blue, she turned to me and said, "There is no hugging allowed." I nodded but I had stood when I saw my parents and I realized, also, I had edged forward towards them. My movement was involuntary, but it had alarmed the support worker and she seemed reluctant to leave. She placed a small electronic timer at the end of our table. She said there was no touching allowed. She asked me not to try and hold my father's hand and said that I was to remain on the opposite side of the plastic divider that ran the length of the table. I told her I would, and I nodded, to show her that I understood and that I would not disobey her orders. She wore a blue facemask and a bandana over her hair, so I could only see her eyes, which were blue and watery, as if she'd been crying. This was the first weekend the care home had been open to visitors in six months. She probably had been crying. "Please, no hugging," she said, once more, as my mother helped settle my father into a folding chair. Then, in almost a whisper, she said, "I've been saying this all day." She sighed and pressed start on the timer before disappearing around the corner.

I waved to my mother and father through the plastic divider, which was oily and flimsy and undulated in the light breeze. This distorted the image of my parents and they looked as if they'd been painted by Francis Bacon, as if they were an abstract portrait of themselves. Even through the rippling plastic I could see that my father was smiling and I could sense his calm contentedness and this was reassuring. My mother was focused on him, fixing his collar, fussing over his hair, directing him to look at me, to say hello, which he did, although I couldn't imagine what he might have seen, how distorted my own image was, or the green swirl of the garden behind me, the parking lot, the sparse, small trees.

We began to speak but the wind shifted and blew the conversation from the next table into our space and we could hear, with crystalline clarity, the ancient farmer whose hearing aids had gone through the wash reciting a litany of harvests past. We couldn't see him, because his table was around the red-brick corner of the building, pushed up against the front wall, and we were tucked around back, but we could hear him as if he was sitting at our table, so we contended with this benign ghost and let his recitation intertwine with our conversation. We had no choice.

"Peas!"

"How are you feeling, Dad?"

"Potatoes!"

"Are you sleeping well?"

"Beans!"

"Dad, can you hear me?"

"Cabbage!"

"Mom, can I can touch his toes? With mine? We're wearing shoes. Will I get in trouble?"

"Corn!"

"I'm going to touch his toes. I don't care. Dad, that's me, I'm tapping your shoe."

"Strawberries!"

"I'll come back next week, Dad. I'll bring the kids. We can draw together."

"Asparagus!"

"Bye Dad, I love you."

"Tomatoes!"

The alarm's beeping ended our strange interwoven talk and let us know that our allotted thirty minutes had ended. There was no way to extend our time because so many people were waiting for their turn to see the people they loved and from whom they'd been separated over the past six months. It seemed impossible to me that those visitors could love their parent or grandparent or whomever they were here to see as much as I loved my father, although I understood that they must. I was not to linger here. The support worker had asked me to make my exit brisk and I didn't want to disappoint her or further exhaust her by causing a weepy scene where I might inadvertently take my father's hand. I didn't stay to watch my mother guide my father through the glass doors of the entrance to the home. Instead, I walked straight towards where my car was parked in the lot, and I didn't turn around, not once. I could not have imagined such a cruel separation at this late stage in my father's life. That he might live in one world and I in another. I had a terrible feeling that if I turned around to have one last look at my dad the spell might be broken and he would return inside and I'd never have the chance to see him again. It wasn't until I'd pulled onto the highway that I realized that by not turning around, I had missed the opportunity to see the ancient farmer who'd been such a large part of our visit. I imagined him as a younger man surveying a field of newly growing crop, a dog with mismatched eyes, one brown, one blue, at his side. I imagined him as an older man on a folding chair, at a banquet table with a plastic divider, although I could see this image of him less clearly. I would never know this man, young or old, but I would remember him. I would remember his enthusiasm, the poetry of his words, and the sound of his voice.

＊

Time is a story that we tell ourselves. It is through our experiences that we create its narrative. Claudia Hammond writes that the experience of time is personal. In a reference to Edmund Husserl's phenomenology of time-consciousness theory, she writes that "we hear a song one note at a time, but it is our sense of the future and the past—our memory and our anticipation—that makes it a song."

The same can be said of stories. We gather them word by word and string them together to form a scene within which we discover characters; sometimes they are people we know, and sometimes they are new to us, and these characters exist in landscapes that seem real but are always imagined, and we trust, based on our knowledge of past stories, that we will learn something new on the journey through this story and, also, that there will be an ending.

*

We were driving through a whiteout. I was in the car with my father, taking him back to the care home where he lived. It was winter, on a dark night in early December, and it was nearly eight o'clock, which was later than I'd promised to return him. Almost as soon as we left the main highway, heading north, a winter storm had over-taken us. It was a sudden, ferocious snow squall. It had been brewing hours before as we'd sat with my mother at the kitchen table in my parents' home, the day's light fading, eating chicken pot pie and drinking cranberry juice instead of wine. Outside the window I'd seen the flakes, innocent and gentle. I'd kept eating.

My father, sitting in the passenger seat beside me, was overstuffed in his layers of cold-weather clothing. My mother had found a vest for him to wear, a two-toned tan and navy puffer, something a lumberjack might wear when chopping firewood. She'd written his name on the inside of the collar in marker so it wouldn't go missing in the care home. She often turned up to discover other men wearing my father's shirts, my father wearing theirs.

She'd zipped him into a second coat and tied a soft tartan scarf around his neck.

"Don't let him go inside with these glasses on," she'd said, sliding a pair of grey spectacles onto my father's nose. They were distance glasses, reserved for car rides so my father could see the details of the passing landscape. Tonight, however, neither of us could see anything at all.

There were no other cars. I could see no headlights in my rear-view mirror, and there were no tracks to follow on the snow-covered road ahead. The snowflakes were coming in on the horizontal, and a persistent westerly gust shook the car. The windshield wipers moved hysterically, and yet they were still not fast enough to clear my view. I tried the car's high beams but instead of illuminating a path forward they created a terrible wall of white light, the reflection of millions of individual flakes, as if each was a mirror. I switched back to the regular headlights, and this had the uneasy effect of lighting only a few feet in front of us. It was as if we were driving through a tunnel. We could have been travelling through the cave to the underworld, we could have been at the bottom of the ocean, we could have been in outer space.

For the duration of the highway ride and into the squall, my father had been instructing me how to drive, which he did every time I drove him back to the care home. Tonight, he was focused mainly on my speed but occasionally he offered directions on which route to follow.

Take your foot off the accelerator and slow down now, okay, slow down, and, now, turn into the other lane and put your indicator on, then, *speed up as fast as you can. You don't need to put your foot on the brake. You just need to take your foot off the accelerator.*

His directions made a vague sort of sense, although I knew I shouldn't follow them. He told me to drive in the opposing lane, and make left or right turns that led to unknown places. He never objected to the fact that I wasn't carrying out his directives.

The landscape along this drive had become familiar to me over the spring and summer. I'd taken many trips to visit my father, and, on a few occasions like this, I'd driven him home after his visits to our cottage. It was a pastoral route, one of rolling green hills and farm fields. One small town had a library with a wraparound porch and a lovely red-brick church. I'd noticed a series of odd signs posted along the way, advertisements that were both direct and obscure and had become markers for my journeys to and from visiting my father. Seeing the *Garage Guru!* sign meant I was almost there but passing *Soil! Soil! Soil!* indicated there was still some time to go.

Once, when I was driving him home last summer, my father had abruptly stopped his driving instructions to show me a lone oak tree on the rise of a hill and how the light was shining through its leaves. "Look at that," he'd marvelled and he'd outlined the shape of the tree with his hand as if he were making a drawing, which, in a way, he was.

Hours before our winter journey, I'd shown my father a trio of his early paintings that were reproduced in a magazine. He'd picked out his favourite (*Enigma*, 1958, now in the National Gallery of Canada) and he'd said, "That's a beauty." Then, he'd pointed to a second painting, one he'd done in his twenties and that he hadn't seen since because it had been sold to a private collector. It was vaguely figurative, and I could make out what might be body parts, but it was mostly abstract. He'd examined the work and he'd said "wrestlers," which is the painting's title, a painting he hadn't seen in sixty years, summoned with clarity, and, I sensed, delight, as if greeting an old friend. It was this sense of delight, I thought, that my father had given me. He has shown me how lucky we are to live in a world so interesting, so inspiring and beautiful—where the light shining through the leaves of a lone oak on a hill was something worth noticing. He'd taught me that the world can be both real and imagined and life can be given and hoped for and you must remember to look, to truly look, and see what is in front of you, and, to see beyond it as well.

✳

One last rule in the Years Thought Days tales is that a mortal who enters the otherworld is able to return to the human world. I had initially overlooked this statement, thinking it was obvious, and overly simplistic. I was wrong, though. It might be the most important rule of all. My dad didn't die on that December night; he came back. He would live only one more year, nearly half of which I would be barred from visiting him, but, another year—of life!—is extraordinary. It is the real magic of this story.

✳

In the storm I could not see the library with the wrap-around porch or the obscure advertising signs or the hills or even a single tree. It was as if the lights of the world had been switched off, and perhaps they had. It was not unthinkable that a power line had gone down in a storm like this. And there we were, my father and me, moving through the impassable, unknowable dark in the steel bullet of my mother's red car. *That's right. A slight turn. Foot off the accelerator. Don't use your brakes. Turn right, now left, put your indicator on.* In that moment the two of us were all that mattered.

"There," my father said. "My God, there it is." He pointed at a shape along the roadside. It was the sign indicating the turn for the city where he now lived. It had been mostly covered by snow but I could see, as I passed slowly by, the first few letters of a familiar street name. I might have been driving on the shoulder of the road, which is why the sign was close enough to see, but it didn't matter. I pulled off to the right and I briefly shone my high beams into the distance where there was a flash of red. It was the stop sign where we would turn left and head up the hill to the care home. How lucky we are, I thought, as the windshield wipers waved frantically back and forth, my grip on the wheel tight, my fingers numb with cold, that we made it, that I will deliver my father safely, and hug him, and say goodbye, and I will wish that life were different and that he could be at home while also understanding that he will be cared for, with kindness, and that after I leave he will be helped into his pyjamas, then into a warm bed with clean sheets where

he will drift off to sleep, and while all of this is happening, I will be back in my mother's red car, in the darkness
of the winter storm, my father's instructions a persistent
comforting echo. Alone, with my memories, I will find
my way home.

Notes

THE MATTER

Piaget, Jean, and Bärbel Inhelder. *The Psychology of the Child: The Definitive Account of the Psychologist's Work.* New York: Basic Books, 2000.

Singer, Dorothy B. and Tracey A. Revenson. *A Piaget Primer: How A Child Thinks.* New York: Plume, 1996.

Britannica, T. Editors of Encyclopaedia. "Jean Piaget." *Encyclopedia Britannica*, September 12, 2021. https://www.britannica.com/biography/Jean-Piaget.

Woolley, Jacqueline D., and Maliki E. Ghossainy. "Revisiting the Fantasy-Reality Distinction: Children as Naïve Skeptics." *Child Development* 84, no. 5 (2013): 1496–1510. https://doi.org/10.1111/cdev.12081.

Woolley, Jacqueline D. "Do you Believe in Surnits?" *New York Times*, Dec. 23, 2006. https://www.nytimes.com/2006/12/23/opinion/23woolley.html

Harris, Paul L., Emma Brown, Crispin Marriott, Semantha Whittall, and Sarah Harmer. "Monsters, Ghosts and Witches: Testing the Limits of the Fantasy-Reality Distinction in Young Children." *British Journal of Developmental Psychology* 9, no. 1 (1991): 105–23. https://doi.org/10.1111/j.2044-835X.1991.tb00865.x.

Vaden, Victoria Cox, and Jacqueline D. Woolley. "Does God Make It Real? Children's Belief in Religious Stories from the

Judeo-Christian Tradition." *Child Development* 82, no. 4 (2011): 1120–35. https://doi.org/10.1111/j.1467-8624.2011.01589.x.

Rosengren, Karl S., and Anne K. Hickling. "Seeing Is Believing: Children's Explanations of Commonplace, Magical, and Extraordinary Transformations." *Child Development* 65, no. 6 (1994): 1605–26. https://doi.org/10.1111/j.1467-8624.1994.tb00838.x.

Woolley, Jacqueline D., and Jennifer Van Reet. "Effects of Context on Judgments Concerning the Reality Status of Novel Entities." *Child Development* 77, no. 6 (2006): 1778–93. https://doi.org/10.1111/j.1467-8624.2006.00973.x.

Woolley, Jacqueline D., and Chelsea A. Cornelius. "Beliefs in Magical Beings and Cultural Myths." In *The Oxford Handbook of the Development of Imagination*. Oxford: Oxford University Press, 2013. https://doi.org/10.1093/oxfordhb/9780195395761.013.0005.

Cornelius, Chelsea A., Walter Lacy, and Jacqueline D. Woolley. "Developmental Changes in the Use of Supernatural Explanations for Unusual Events." *Journal of Cognition and Culture* 11, no. 3–4 (2011): 311–37. https://doi.org/10.1163/156853711X591279.

Johnson, Carl N., and Paul L. Harris. "Magic: Special But Not Excluded." *British Journal of Developmental Psychology* 12, no. 1 (1994): 35–51. https://doi.org/10.1111/j.2044-835X.1994.tb00617.x.

Edwards, Kathryn A. "The History of Ghosts in Early Modern Europe: Recent Research and Future Trajectories." *History Compass* 10, no. 4 (2012): 353–66. https://doi.org/10.1111/j.1478-0542.2012.00840.x.

Goldstein, Diane. "Scientific Rationalism and Supernatural Experience Narratives." In *Haunting Experiences, Ghosts in Contemporary Folklore*, eds. Jeannie Banks Thomas, Sylvia Grider, and Diane Logan Goldstein. Utah: Utah State University Press, 2007.

Thomas, Jeannie Banks. "The Usefulness of Ghost Stories." In *Haunting Experiences, Ghosts in Contemporary Folklore*, eds. Jeannie Banks Thomas, Sylvia Grider, and Diane Logan Goldstein. Utah: Utah State University Press, 2007.

Grider, Sylvia. "Children's Ghost Stories." In *Haunting Experiences, Ghosts in Contemporary Folklore*, eds. Jeannie Banks Thomas, Sylvia Grider, and Diane Logan Goldstein. Utah: Utah State University Press, 2007.

Morison, Patricia, and Howard Gardner. "Dragons and Dinosaurs: The Child's Capacity to Differentiate Fantasy from Reality." Child Development 49, no. 3 (1978): 642–48. https://doi.org/10.1111/j.1467-8624.1978.tb02364.x.

Donaldson, Julia. The Paper Dolls. London: MacMillan, 2012.

LESSONS FOR FEMALE SUCCESS

Sargent, Helen Child, and George Lyman Kittredge, eds. English and Scottish Popular Ballads. Boston: Houghton Mifflin, 1965.

Stewart, Polly. "Wishful Willful Wily Women: Lessons for Female Success in the Child Ballads." In Feminist Messages: Coding in Women's Folk Culture, ed. Joan Newlon Radner. Urbana: University of Illinois Press, 1993.

Burton, Thomas G. Some Ballad Folks. Johnson City, Tennessee: East Tennessee State University Research Development Committee, 1978.

Garber, Megan. "The Bittersweet Lessons of Law & Order: SVU." The Atlantic, December 2, 2019. https://www.theatlantic.com/entertainment/archive/2019/12/watching-law-order-svu-first-time/602686/ .

Nussbaum, Emily. "Trauma Queen: The pulp appeal of Law & Order: SVU." The New Yorker, June 10, 2013. https://www.newyorker.com/magazine/2013/06/10/trauma-queen.

Moreira, James. "Ballad." In Folklore: An Encyclopedia of Beliefs, Customs, Tales, Music, and Art, ed. Thomas A. Green. Santa Barbara: ABC-CLIO, 1997.

CHIMERA

Hulubaş, Adina. "Romanian beliefs and rites of pregnancy with special reference to Moldova, folklore." Folklore 122, no. 3 (2011): 264–282. https://doi.org/10.1080/0015587X.2011.608264.

Rijnink, E. C., et al. "Tissue microchimerism is increased during pregnancy: a human autopsy study." Molecular Human Reproduction 21, no. 11 (2015): 857–64. https://doi.org/10.1093/molehr/gav047.

Van de Groot, F.R.W., and R. L. ten Berge. "Lamashtu, 'she who erases,' touched her stomach seven times to kill the child." Journal of Clinical Pathology 55, no. 7 (2002): 534. https://doi.org/10.1136/jcp.55.7.534

Kruk, Remke. "Pregnancy and Its Social Consequences in Mediaeval and Traditional Arab Society." Quaderni Di Studi

Arabi 5/6 (1987): 418–30. http://www.jstor.org/stable/25802620.

Fitzgerald, Daniel W., and Frieda M. T. F. Behets. "Beyond Folklore." *Journal of the American Medical Association* 288, no. 22 (2002): 2791–2792.

Moto-Sanchez, Milla Micka. "Jizō, Healing Rituals, and Women in Japan." *Japanese Journal of Religious Studies* 43, no. 2 (2016): 307–31.

Murphy, E. M. "Children's Burial Grounds in Ireland (Cillíní) and Parental Emotions Toward Infant Death." *International Journal of Historical Archaeology* 15, no. 3, 409–428. https://doi.org/10.1007/s10761-011-0148-8.

Harrison, Elizabeth G., and Igeta Midori. "Women's Responses to Child Loss in Japan: The Case of 'Mizuko Kuyō' [with Response]." *Journal of Feminist Studies in Religion* 11, no. 2 (1995): 67–100. http://www.jstor.org/stable/25002258.

Harrison, Elizabeth G. "Strands of Complexity: The Emergence of 'Mizuko Kuyō' in Postwar Japan." *Journal of the American Academy of Religion* 67, no. 4 (1999): 769–96. http://www.jstor.org/stable/1466269.

Schmiesing, Ann. "Naming the Helper: Maternal Concerns and the Queen's Incorrect Guesses in the Grimms' 'Rumpelstiltskin.'" *Marvels & Tales* 25, no. 2 (2011): 298–315. http://www.jstor.org/stable/41389005.

Arden, Rosalind, et al. "Genes influence young children's human figure drawings and their association with intelligence a decade later." *Psychological Science* 25, no. 10 (2014): 1843–50. https://doi.org/10.1177/0956797614540686.

ORDINARY WONDER TALES

Propp, Vladimir. *Morphology of the Folktale*. Austin: University of Texas Press, 1968.

Olrik, Axel. "Epic Laws of Folk Narrative." In *The Study of Folklore*, edited by Alan Dundes, 129–41. Englewood Cliffs, N.J.: Prentice-Hall, 1965.

CHILD UNWITTINGLY PROMISED

Ranke, Kurt, ed. trans. Lotte Baumann. *Folktales of Germany*. Translated by Lotte Baumann. Chicago: University of Chicago Press, 1966.

Seki, Keigo, ed. Trans. Robert J Adams. *Folktales of Japan*. Translated by Robert J. Adams. Chicago: University of Chicago Press, 1963.

Grimm, Wilhelm and Jacob. *The Complete Fairy Tales of the Brothers*

Grimm, ed. Jack Zipes. New York: Bantam Classics, 1987.

Paradiz, Valerie. *Clever Maids: The Secret History of the Grimm Fairy Tales*. New York: Basic Books, 2009.

de Blécourt, Willem. "On the origin of 'Hänsel und Gretel.'" *Fabula* 49, no. 1 (2008): 30–46.

de Blécourt, Willem. *Tales of Magic, Tales in Print: On the Genealogy of Fairy Tales and the Brothers Grimm*. Manchester: Manchester University Press, 2012.

Thum, Maureen. "Feminist or Anti-Feminist? Gender-Coded Role Models in the Tales Contributed by Dorothea Viehmann to the Grimm Brothers 'Kinder- und Hausmärchen.' *Germanic Review* 68, no. 1 (1993): 11. https://doi.org/10.1080/00168890.1993.9934217

GIVING UP THE GHOST

Kübler-Ross, Elizabeth, and David Kessler. *On Grief and Grieving: Finding the meaning of grief through the five stages of loss*. New York: Scribner, 2014.

Castelnovo, Anna, et al. "Post-bereavement hallucinatory experiences: A critical overview of population and clinical studies." *Journal of Affective Disorders* 186 (2015): 266–74. https://doi.org/10.1016/j.jad.2015.07.032.

MacDonald, William L. "Idionecrophanies: The Social Construction of Perceived Contact with the Dead." *Journal for the Scientific Study of Religion* 31, no. 2 (1992): 215–23. https://www.jstor.org/stable/1387010

Grimby, A. "Bereavement among elderly people: grief reactions, post-bereavement hallucinations and quality of life." *Acta Psychiatrica Scandinavica* 87, no. 1 (1993): 72–80. https://doi.org/10.1177/1363461520962887

Matchett, W. F. "Repeated hallucinatory experiences as a part of the mourning process among Hopi Indian women." *Psychiatry* 35, no. 2 (1972): 185–94. https://doi.org/10.1080/00332747.1972.11023711

Baethge, Christopher. "Grief hallucinations: true or pseudo? Serious or not? An inquiry into psychopathological and clinical features of a common phenomenon." *Psychopathology* 35, no. 5 (2002): 296–302.

Kalish, Richard A., and David K. Reynolds. "Phenomenological Reality and Post-Death Contact." *Journal for the Scientific Study* of *Religion* 12, no. 2 (1973): 209–21.

Jakoby, Nina R. "Grief as a Social Emotion: Theoretical Perspectives." *Death Studies* 36, no. 8 (2012): 679–711.

Larøi, Frank, et al. "Culture and hallucinations: overview and future directions." *Schizophrenia bulletin* 40, no. 4 (2014): 213–20.

Lindow, John. *Swedish Legends and Folktales*. Berkeley: University of California Press, 1978.

Kvideland, Reimund, and Henry K. Sehmsdorf, eds. *Scandinavian Folk Belief and Legend*. Minneapolis: University of Minesota Press, 1991.

Sacks, Oliver. *Hallucinations*. New York: Vintage, 2013.

Pies, Ronald W. "The Bereavement Exclusion and DSM-5: An Update and Commentary." *Innovations in Clinical Neuroscience* 11: 7–8 (2014): 19–22.

Parkes, C. M. "Bereavement in adult life." *British Medical Journal* 316: 7134 (1998): 856–9. doi:10.1136/bmj.316.7134.856.

Ryall, Julian. "Taxi drivers in Tsunami Disaster Zone report Ghost Passengers." *The Telegraph*, January 21, 2016. https://www.telegraph.co.uk/news/worldnews/asia/japan/12111749/Taxi-drivers-in-tsunami-disaster-zone-report-ghost-passengers.html.

Khan, Maria. "Japan Taxi Drivers Pick up Ghost Passengers in Tsunami-Hit Towns." *International Business Times*, January 21, 2016. https://www.ibtimes.co.uk/japan-taxi-drivers-pick-ghost-passengers-tsunami-hit-towns-1539387.

Yama, Megumi. "The Meaning of Mystical Experiences on the Boundary Between Life and Death: Observations from Survivors of the Great East Japan Earthquake." *Jung Journal* 13, no. 2 (2019): 21–34. https://doi.org/10.1080/19342039.2019.1600978.

Yama, Megumi. "The Meaning of Mystical Experiences on the Boundary between Life and Death." *Jung Journal* 13, no. 2 (2019): 21–34. doi:10.1080/19342039.2019.1600978.

McCarthy-Jones, Simon. "Sensing the Dead is Perfectly Normal and Often Helpful." *The Conversation*. July 19, 2017. https://theconversation.com/sensing-the-dead-is-perfectly-normal-and-often-helpful-81048.

Sherman, Josepha. "Ajok." In *Storytelling: An Encyclopedia of Mythology and Folklore*. London: Routlege, 2015.

Lynch, Patricia Ann, and Jeremy Roberts. "Ajok." In *African*

Mythology, A to Z. New York: Infobase Publishing, 2010.

Cotterell, Arthur. "Ajok." In The Oxford Dictionary of World Mythology. Oxford: Oxford University Press, 1986.

NUCLEAR FOLKLORE

Cohen, Paul. "AECB pays for house to be torn down on Dorset Street," Port Hope Evening Guide, Wednesday, December 7, 1977.

Sanger, Penny. Blind Faith: The Nuclear Industry in One Small Town. Toronto: McGraw-Hill Ryerson, 1981.

"Town Story," Port Hope History. http://porthopehistory.com/townstory/.

Cutting, James. "Second Eldorado Leak into Town Harbour," Port Hope Evening Guide, date unknown.

"Radioactive Storage at Town Park," Port Hope Evening Guide, June 27, 1978.

Keating, Michael. "Eldorado Charged with Polluting Lake," Port Hope Evening Guide, November 11, 1979.

"Radioactive waste," Canadian Nuclear Safety Commission Historic Waste Management Program. http://nuclearsafety.gc.ca/eng/waste/index.cfm.

"Historic nuclear waste," Canadian Nuclear Safety Commission, November 11, 2021.

http://nuclearsafety.gc.ca/eng/waste/historic-nuclear-waste/index.cfm.

Radiological Property File of 150 Dorset Street Port Hope, Ontario, Atomic Energy Control Board of Canada, now Canadian Nuclear Safety Commission. Access to Information request filed 2014.

Northumberland Land Registry Files for Lot 66 (150 Dorset Street). Northumberland Land Registry Office, Cobourg, Ontario, 2017.

"Radioactive Century-Old house Mystifies Experts," Globe and Mail, June 20, 1977.

"AECB refuses radiation information," Greg Bannister, Peterborough Examiner, date unknown.

"Chief Chemist Retires," Inco Triangle, November 1944, 15.

"Talented Artist," Inco Triangle, November 1938, 4.

"Canada's historical role in developing nuclear weapons," Canadian Nuclear Safety Commission, May 28, 2012. https://

nuclearsafety.gc.ca/eng/resources/fact-sheets/Canadas-contribution-to-nuclear-weapons-development.cfm.

"Canada's nuclear history," Canadian Nuclear Safety Commission, March 3, 2017. https://nuclearsafety.gc.ca/eng/resources/canadas-nuclear-history/index.cfm.

Nixon, Alan. *Canada's Nuclear Fuel Industry: An Overview.* Science and Technology Division, Government of Canada Publications, November 1993. https://publications.gc.ca/Collection-R/LoPBdP/BP/bp360-e.htm.

Port Hope High School Yearbook, 1972–1973 and 1973–1974.

"Radon Gas: It's in your home," Government of Canada Publications. https://www.canada.ca/en/health-canada/services/environmental-workplace-health/reports-publications/radiation/radon-your-home-health-canada-2009.html.

Jorgenson, Tim. *Strange Glow: The Story of Radiation.* Princeton: Princeton University Press, 2017.

Rose, Doreen. Letter. Jane Urquhart fonds. Library and Archives Canada.

Rose, Doreen. Rose Doreen to Jane Urquhart, December 1977. Library and Archives Canada.

Tilman, Anna, John Jacksohn, and Irene Kock. *Great Lakes Region Nuclear Hotspots* (map), Citizens Clearinghouse on Waste Management and Great Lakes United. February 2016.

"Port Hope: Area of Concern," Environment Canada Areas of Concern, February 13, 2017. https://www.canada.ca/en/environment-climate-change/services/great-lakes-protection/areas-concern/port-hope.html.

"Lake Ontario Drainage Basin," Environment Canada. February 27, 2017. https://www.canada.ca/en/environment-climate-change/services/great-lakes-protection/maps/lake-ontario-drainage-basin.html.

"Coast guard investigates unknown sheen in lake Ontario," AP *News*, June 26, 2018, https://apnews.com/article/1e8267d-4c93b4f37b43706f1b44c82cc.

"Lake Ontario," *Waterkeeper.* http://www.waterkeeper.ca/lake-ontario/.

"Fact Sheet: Protecting the Great Lakes from Radionuclides," Canadian Nuclear Safety Commission. June 2016, https://publications.gc.ca/site/eng/9.819988/publication.html.

PHAI (Port Hope Area Initiative). https://www.phai.ca/.

"The Cosmic Origins of Uranium," World Nuclear Association, updated April 2021. https://www.world-nuclear.org/information-library/nuclear-fuel-cycle/uranium-resources/the-cosmic-origins-of-uranium.aspx.

"What is a Supernova?" National Aeronautics and Space Administration, September 4, 2013. https://www.nasa.gov/audience/forstudents/5-8/features/nasa-knows/what-is-a-supernova.html.

"Association of Assessment of the Relevance of the Inclusion of Radionuclides as a Chemical of Mutual Concern under Annex 3 of the Canada-United States Great Lakes Water Quality Agreement," Canadian Nuclear Safety Commission, updated April 3, 2014. Association of Assessment of the Relevance of the Inclusion of Radionuclides as a Chemical of Mutual Concern under Annex 3 of the Canada-United States Great Lakes Water Quality Agreement. http://nuclearsafety.gc.ca/eng/resources/health/radionuclides-chemical-of-mutual-concern.cfm.

"Health effects of the Chernobyl accident and special health care programmes: Report of the UN Chernobyl Forum Expert Group 'Health,'" World Health Organization, May 1, 2006. https://www.who.int/publications/i/item/9241594179.

Additional information for this essay came from email, telephone, and in-person interviews with the following people:

Maude-Émilie Pagé, Director of Communications and Government Reporting, Atomic Energy of Canada Limited

Sandy Holmes, Community Relations Coordinator, Port Hope Area Initiative Management Office

Shernette Muccuth Henry, Communications Officer, Historic Waste Program Management Office, Canadian Nuclear Laboratories

Also,

John Carter, Lee Caswell, Paul Evans, Ilona Kirby, Timothy Jorgenson, and Tom Sills

THE PLAGUE LEGENDS

Kvideland, Reimund, and Henry K. Sehmsdorf, eds. Scandinavian Folk Belief and Legend. Minneapolis: University of Minesota Press, 1991.

Tangherlini, Timothy R. "Ships, Fogs, and Traveling Pairs:

Plague Legend Migration in Scandinavia." *The Journal of American Folklore* 101, no. 400 (1988): 176–206. https://doi.org/10.2307/540108.

Hiiemäe, Reet. "Mapping the trajectories of the plague spirit: a case study of handling collective fear." Folklore: Electronic Journal of Folklore, 26 (2004): 65-80. https://doi:10.7592/FEJF2004.26.hiiemae

Lindow, John. *Swedish Legends and Folktales*. Berkeley: University of California Press, 1978.

Ranke, Kurt, ed. trans. Lotte Baumann. *Folktales of Germany*. Translated by Lotte Baumann. Chicago: University of Chicago Press, 1966.

Dahlmann, La. "Folktales, Pesta and the Black Death." *Talk Norway*.https://talknorway.no/folk-tales-pesta-and-the-black-death-norway/.

Tangherlini, Timothy R. "'It Happened Not Too Far from Here …': A Survey of Legend Theory and Characterization." *Western Folklore* 49, no. 4 (1990): 371–90. https://doi.org/10.2307/1499751.

Dégh, Linda, and Andrew Vázsonyi. "The Memorate and the Proto-Memorate." *The Journal of American Folklore* 87, no. 345 (1974): 225–39. https://doi.org/10.2307/538735.

Dégh, Linda. "What Is a Belief Legend?" *Folklore* 107 (1996): 33–46. http://www.jstor.org/stable/1260912.

Honko, Lauri. "Memorates and the Study of Folk Beliefs." *Journal of the Folklore Institute* 1, no. 1–2 (1964): 5–19. https://doi.org/10.2307/3814027.

Christiansen, Reidar Thoralf. "The migratory legends: a proposed list of types with a systematic catalogue of the Norwegian variants." *FF Communications* 175. Helsinki: The Finish Academy of Science and Letters, 1958.

Furukawa Y, and R. Kansaku. "Amabié—A Japanese Symbol of the COVID-19 Pandemic." *Journal of the American Medical Association* 324, no. 6 (2020): 531–533. doi:10.1001/jama.2020.12660.

Merli, Claudia. "A chimeric being from Kyushu, Japan: Amabie's revival during Covid-19." *Anthropology Today* 36, no. 5 (2020): 6–10. doi:10.1111/1467-8322.12602.

YEARS THOUGHT DAYS

Fujii, Masahiko, et al. "A Japanese fairy tale, Urashima Taro, and dementia." *Psychogeriatrics: the official journal of the Japanese Psychogeriatric Society* 15, no. 4 (2015): 279–80. doi:10.1111/psyg.12123.

Hammond, Claudia. *Time Warped: Unlocking the Mysteries of Time Perception.* Toronto: House of Anansi, 2012.

Klein, Stefan. *The Secret Pulse of Time: Making Sense of Life's Scarcest Commodity.* Cambridge: Marlowe & Company, 2007.

Ogden, R. S. "The passage of time during the UK Covid-19 lock-down." PLoS ONE 15, no. 7 2020. https://doi.org/10.1371/journal.pone.0235871

Lepage, Martin, Reza Habib, and Endel Tulving. "Hippocampal PET activations of memory encoding and retrieval: the HIPER model." *Hippocampus* 8, no. 4 (1998): 313-322.

Glassie, Henry. *Irish Folk Tales.* New York: Pantheon Books, 1987.

Mencej, Mirjam. "Spaces of Passage into Supernatural Time." *Tautosakos Darbai / Folklore Studies* 44 (2012): 30–48.

Jason, Heda. *Ethnopoetry: Form, Content, Function.* Bonn: Linguistica Biblica, 1977.

Kaasik, Mairi. "A Mortal Visits the Other World – The Relativity of Time in Estonian Fairy Tales." *Journal of Ethnology and Folkloristics* 7, no. 2 (2013), 33–47.

Holbek, Bengt. *The Interpretation of Fairy Tales: Danish Folklore in a European Perspective.* Helsinki: Suomalainen Tiedeakatemia, 1987.

Aarne, Antti. *The Types of the Folktale: A Classification and Bibliography,* Helsinki: The Finnish Academy of Science and Letters, 1961.

Uther, Hans-Jörg. "The Types of International Folktales: A Classification and Bibliography. Based on the system of Antti Aarne and Stith Thompson." FF Communications 284–286. Helsinki: The Finish Academy of Science and Letters, 2004.

Conrad, JoAnn. "The Storied Time of Folklore." *Western Folklore* 73, no. 2–3 (2014): 323–52. http://www.jstor.org/stable/24550978.

El Haj, Mohamed, and Frank Larøi. "Confabulations on Time: Relationship between Confabulations and Timing Deviations in Alzheimer's Disease." *Archives of Clinical Neuropsychology* 35 (2020): 377–384.

Morrissey, Kellie. "'Time travel' as dementia care is spreading, but the future may be more powerful than the past." *The Conversation,* July 29, 2019. https://theconversation.com/profiles/kellie-morrissey-778446.

Ricoeur, Paul. "Narrative Time." *Critical Inquiry* 7, no. 1 (1980): 169–90. http://www.jstor.org/stable/1343181.

Acknowledgements

A LIST IN ALPHABETICAL ORDER

ALL: Thank you to all the people that agreed to be interviewed for this book, and all the people who spoke with me about this book and offered advice and input, and thank you to everyone I have forgotten to mention. Even if unnamed, please know that you live here in these pages.

ART: Byron Eggenschwiler illustrated a story I wrote ten years ago and I loved it so much I bought three of the prints. It was an image of my daughter, but, I'd have loved it regardless. The creative folks at Bilbioasis asked my opinion on cover design, and more as a wish than a request I suggested that Eggenschwiler do the job. And they asked him! And he said yes! I adore this cover and will soon be ordering prints of it to hang on my wall. Enormous thanks to Byron and to Vanessa Stauffer for making this wish come true.

BIBLIOASIS: Dan Wells intuited what I wanted for this collection of essays and allowed me the freedom and editorial guidance to get there. It is a much better, focused book for his involvement. Vanessa Stauffer offered early encouragement when I most needed it and carried the book all the way through to the finished product. Thank you to Cat London for her copy-editing magic, and to Emily Stephenson-Bowes and Ashley Van Elswyk for their promotional efforts and to the rest of the Biblioasis staff. It was been a pleasure and an honour working with all of you.

CAMARADERIE: Carrie Snyder and Tasneem Jamal offered wisdom, editorial advice, friendship, chocolate and weird beer and I couldn't have written this book without them.

FAMILY: Thanks to Andrew for sustenance and inspiration, for listening to early drafts read aloud, and for showing me the wonders of the natural world. Also, thanks for taking the kids on long bike rides when I had a deadline. I'm grateful to our children Sadie and Rory for being interesting and curious and ridiculous and pushing me outside my comfort zone in the best of ways.

HOUSES: Kind people offered me their spaces to work in. This includes Krista Blake, Don and Mary Lou Trant, and Beth MacIntosh and Christian Snyder.

MAGAZINES: There are few venues for longform nonfiction and I am grateful to have published earlier versions of some of these essays in magazines and journals. I'd like to acknowledge the editors who worked on these pieces, from whom I learned a great deal. This includes Robbie

Maakestad at The Rumpus ("Lessons for Female Success"), Arielle Spence at Room Magazine ("Chimera"), Amanda Feinman at Guernica ("The Plague Legends"), Sari Botton at Longreads ("Giving up the Ghost"), Pamela Mulloy at The New Quarterly ("Child Unwittingly Promised"), Curtis Gillespie at 18 Bridges ("Nuclear Folklore") and Margaret Nowacyk at The American Journal of Medical Genetics (some aspects of the story "Clairvoyance" appear in "Child Unwittingly Promised").

REPRESENTATION: Samantha Haywood's continued presence in my life is a gift. Sometimes when I am dealing with a difficult situation I try to channel her calm demeanour and practical approach. I'll never live up to the real thing but I will keep taking notes every time we connect.

SUPPORT: I began working on this book while working as Wilfrid Laurier University's Edna Staebler Writer in Residence. To complete this collection I received funding from the Ontario Arts Council, the Canada Council for the Arts, and the Region of Waterloo Arts Fund. For the story "Nuclear Folklore" I received financial support and mentorship via Frontline: Environmental Reportage, a residency at the Banff Centre for the Arts, with guidance from Curtis Gillespie, Sarah Musgrave and Naomi Klein, as well as the other residency participants whose environmental writing was both inspiring and courageous.

URQUHARTS: My sister, Robin Urquhart, and my mother, Jane Urquhart, helped look after my children while I was in Banff, and I'm thankful because this allowed the trip to happen. My mom also helped inform the content of these essays by supplying details about my childhood ghost and other historical facts from our shared past. It still feels unimaginable as I write this, but my dad, Tony Urquhart, died a month after I finished writing this book. These are the last stories I wrote while he was still alive. He provided much of the inspiration and material for the story, *Years Thought Days*, and I wish he was able to read it. His encouragement of my creative work was unwavering and allowed me to wander into the otherworld, which, it turns out, is my true home.

EMILY URQUHART is a journalist with a doctorate in folklore from Memorial University of Newfoundland. Her work has appeared in *Longreads*, *Guernica*, and *The Walrus*, among other publications, and has won a National Magazine Award and an Alberta Magazine Award. Her first book was shortlisted for the Kobo First Book Prize and the BC National Award for Canadian Nonfiction. Her most recent book, *The Age of Creativity: Art, Memory, my Father and Me*, was listed as a top book of 2020 by CBC, NOW *Magazine* and *Quill & Quire*. She is a nonfiction editor for *The New Quarterly* and lives in Kitchener, Ontario.